A Layman's Commentary
On
Ecclesiastes

Marvin (Bud) Sartain

A Layman's Commentary
On
Ecclesiastes

Marvin (Bud) Sartain

Scripture quotations are taken
from the King James version.

PUBLISHED BY:
BRENTWOOD CHRISTIAN PRESS
4000 BEALLWOOD AVENUE
COLUMBUS, GEORGIA 31904

Introduction

The Author believes the book of Ecclesiastes is not an easy book to understand, but also believes that "All Scripture is given by inspiration of God, and is profitable for doctrine, for reproof, for correction, for instruction in righteousness." II Tim. 3:16. These studies in Ecclesiastes are not meant to be a theological treatise; but rather an easy to understand interpretation of Holy Writ. The Author has been an ordained Independent Fundamental Baptist Preacher for 40 years; and approaches all study of scripture according to the exhortation of Paul to Timothy, in II Tim. 2:15. He said, "Study to show thyself approved unto God, a workman that needeth not to be ashamed, rightly dividing the word of truth." I believe that Scripture must be interpreted by other Scripture, lest all men be found liars. If you cannot prove what you preach, from the Bible, don't preach it. In Ecclesiastes there are 12 chapters, 222 verses, and in these studies, you will find over 1600 reference Scriptures, from Genesis to Revelation. To God be the glory.

M.J. (Bud) Sartain
March 23, 1998
Bethel Baptist Church
Irving, Texas

Dedication

This book is dedicated first to the Divine Godhead, Father, Son, and Holy Spirit. Secondly, to the faithful members of Bethel Baptist Church, who sat through 2 1/2 years of Wednesday night Bible study. Last, but not least, this book is dedicated to my dear wife, Martha, who spent long hours typing the manuscript, and has stood at my side and encouraged me for 49 years. Proverbs 18:22 tells us, "Whoso findeth a wife findeth a good thing, and obtaineth favour with God." My "good thing" has helped me to find favour with God for many years.

M.J. Sartain
Bethel Baptist Church
Irving, Texas

Foreword

I am proud to write the foreword to the Book of Ecclesiastes, written by Rev. M.J. Sartain.

I have worked with him at Calvary Baptist Church in Yakima, Washington and have known him since 1958. Every message I have heard him preach has been scholarly, scriptural and Spirit filled. I have used much of his material on Ecclesiastes, and have found it to be some of the greatest help I've ever had. He has taken this most deep book and made it alive for us today.

For the busy Pastor or for the student of the Word of God, that would want to know the vanity of trying to live this life without God, I would recommend this book. For the one that wants to be made aware of the blessings of what we have by trusting in the Lord, I would recommend this book. For the Pastor who wants material that will bless and compliment his ministry, and encourage his people, this book is a must.

Not only is M.J. Sartain my long time friend, but he is a faithful Pastor and a scholar of the Word of God.

I have taught this material in our Adult Sunday School and I have been greatly encouraged by our members, who have told me what it has meant to them. Some who have been Christians for years, have told me they have never had a Pastor teach this special book. They have also told me, in their personal Bible study and devotions that this has been a book they've had a hard time understanding, but this book helps to bring it alive. I will use it and encourage my Pastor friends to do the same.

Pastor T.J. Smith
Harvest Baptist Church
Albany, Oregon

Studies In Ecclesiastes

Introduction

The word Ecclesiastes comes from the Greek word "eklesia," which means: assembly, congregation, or church. The word preacher (found seven times in this book, and only four other places in the entire Bible) means: one who addresses the assembly. *Rom. 10:14.* Paul tells us he was "ordained a preacher" in *I Tim. 2:7*, and again in *II Tim.1:11* he said, "Whereunto I am appointed a preacher, and an apostle, and a teacher of the Gentiles."

I. WHO IS THE AUTHOR OF ECCLESIASTES?
1. Most Bible scholars believe Solomon wrote this book, along with Proverbs and Song of Solomon. Solomon was the youngest son of David and Bathsheba, according to *I Chron. 3:1-5.*
2. In *Eccl. 1:1*, we have these words, "The words of the preacher, the son of David, king in Jerusalem."
3. In *Prov. 1:1* we find this statement, "The proverbs of Solomon the son of David, king in Israel."

II. WHEN WAS ECCLESIASTES WRITTEN?
1. History tells us Solomon was the only son of David who reigned over Israel from Jerusalem. The author himself mentions this in *chapter 1 verse 12,* so we can approximate the time of the writing of this book, between 977 and 935 B.C. Read *I Kings 11:41-43.*
2. C.I. Scofield says 977 B.C. and Thomas Nelson says 935 B.C., so it is probably between those two dates.

III. WHAT IS THE THEME OF ECCLESIASTES?
1. The key word is "VANITY" (found 37 times) in this book, and represents man "under the sun" (found 29

times), trying to find purpose and direction for his life, apart from the Son of God.

2. We know, however, that apart from God, there-is no hope for man; and this is the conclusion of the writer in *Eccl. 12;13-14.*

3. Wisdom comes from God. *Eccl. 2;26.* Chapter 7 verse 12 tells us that "... wisdom giveth life to them that have it." *James 1:5* says. "If any of you lack wisdom, let him ask of God, that giveth to all men liberally, and upbraideth not; and it shall be given him." This is another prominent word in the book of Ecclesiastes.

4. Another theme of this great little book is for man to get the greatest enjoyment from this life, that he can find. Jesus said in *John 10:10,* "... I am come that they might have life, and that they might have it more abundantly."

5. If you are not enjoying the "ABUNDANT LIFE" whose fault is it? Has God let you down?

6. We will find the abundant life when we put Christ at the very center of every undertaking.

7. This book tells us that God wants us to enjoy life here, "under the sun." *Eccl. 2:24-26; 3:12-13; and 22; 5:18-20; 8:15.*

Chapter 1

We discussed *V-I* in the introduction; and believe it identifies the author as Solomon, who was the only son of David who was king from (or who ruled from) Jerusalem. He re-affirms this in *V-12*.

V-2.   "*Vanity*" comes from the word *Vain*. It means; empty, worthless, conceited, and an inflated ego.According to *Psa. 39:5-6, Psa. 62:9* we are all affected with this malady. WITH SOME, IT IS AN INCURABLE DISEASE.

Again in *Psa. 94:11* David said, "*The Lord knoweth the thoughts of man, that they are vanity.*"

The words vanity and vanities are found almost 100 times in the Bible (I counted 93); and not one time is it used in a good or positive sense.

Let's explore the MEANING OF THIS WORD, FURTHER.

1. The main theme of this book is; that apart from God, ALL things done here on earth, "under the sun," is vanity.

2. Again we emphasize, that apart from God, the labor of a man accomplishes nothing, that he takes with him at death. *Isa. 64:6.*

    A. This is the reason there are no pockets in shrouds.

    B. That is why there are no U-Hauls following the hearse to the cemetery.

3. All that is done here "under the sun," is only a beginning and a vanishing away again, repeating itself in a never ending circle.

4. Here is a preacher that had been a king, and it seems, he is speaking from personal experience.

5. In the N.T. we have Paul and Peter, both warning against vanity. In *Eph. 4:17* Paul said, "*This I say therefore, and testify in the Lord, that ye henceforth walk not as other Gentiles walk, in the VANITY of their mind.*"

6. Peter said in *II Pet. 2:18*, where he is warning against false teachers (whose words, C.I. Scofield said are learned and pretentious), "*For when they speak great swelling words of vanity, they allure through the lusts of the flesh, through much wantoness, those that were clean escaped from them who live in error.*"

V-3. The word "profit" here, means, what is left over after man has worked ceaselessly all of his life. What does he have left to show for it that will precede him to heaven? We are not speaking of material things. Remember the words of our Lord, when he said in *Matt. 16:26*, "*For what is a man profited, if he shall gain the whole world, and lose his own soul? or what shall a man give in exchange for his soul?*"

How true the words, "One life to live twill soon be past, ONLY what's done for Christ will last." We can transfer no earthly possessions to heaven, but we can win the lost and disciple them for Christ. That will last throughout eternity.

Remember, we are still on the subject of vanity, which means that whatever is accomplished apart from God is vain. In the next few verses, the Preacher is going to give us some illustrations of "vanity" from creation.

V-4. "*One generation passeth away, and another generation cometh:*"

When one generation passes off the scene, the next one is no different from the previous one, as far as vanity is concerned. WHY? Because the essential nature of man never changes, apart from God. *Psa. 51:5*, "Behold, I was shapen in iniquity; and in sin did my mother conceive me." Read *Isa. 1:5-6; Eccl. 8:11.*

"... but the earth abideth forever."

Here the preacher is simply contrasting the transitory nature of man with the permanent nature of the earth. There will always be an earth. Not this particular one, but an earth nevertheless. We are told this in *Psa. 104:5* and *Psa. 119:90*. Now compare these scriptures with *II Pet. 3:8-13*. Are there any contradictions between these two concepts? Absolutely not! In Peters letter, the earth is cleansed by fire and renovated and made new, but the mass which we call the globe, will remain. Let me illustrate: When we renovated the parsonage, we took everything out of the inside and the outside. When we finished, the house was larger, new inside and out. No one had ever seen this house as it now appears. So it will be with the earth. When we finished the house, there was more new material than old, therefore the house was new.

V-5.   *"The sun also ariseth, ..."*

Man is like the sun. The sun rises and sets every day, and never rests. It has only stopped one time since it was hung in space, and that was to honor God's man. Read *Josh. 10:12-14*. By the way, man is still trying to understand Joshua's long day.

"... and the sun goeth down, and hasteth to his place where he arose."

The sun works in the same orbit that God put it in at creation; it never changes. The sun never progresses from one stage to another; so the old fleshly nature never changes. Only God can change the nature of humanity, according to *II Pet. 1:3-4*. Here Peter tells us, we are partakers of His Divine nature. *II Cor. 5:17* tells us that all things become new, including our nature. *Eph. 4:24* exhorts us to, "Put on the new man, which after God is created in righteousness and true holiness." *Col. 3:10*, "And have put on the new man, which is renewed in knowledge after the image of him that created him."

15

V-6.   *"The wind goeth toward the south, and turneth about unto the north; it whirleth about continually,"*

The wind, on the other hand, is ever changing its course; always circling and blowing in all directions, exhausting every possibility of rest.

"... and the wind returneth again according to his circuits."

WHY? Because it is directed by a higher source of power than its own. The Bible tells us that the fleshly nature of man is influenced by evil forces at work in the world. *Eph. 6:12,* "For we wrestle not against flesh and blood, but against principalities, against powers, against the rulers of darkness of this world, against spiritual wickedness in high places."

"Vanity of vanities, saith the Preacher, vanity of vanities; all is vanity." *Eccl. 1:2.*

We are still on the subject of the vicious cycle of restless humanity. We have seen the sun and wind used as examples of man's never-ending quest for something new; yet the old nature never changes. In *V-7,* God uses the streams as an illustration of the same thing.

V-7.   *"All the rivers run into the sea;"*

Here in the United States, they either run into the Atlantic or the Pacific Ocean.

1. God designed the earth perfectly, and surrounded it with water.

2. For instance; here in the U.S.A., there is the Continental Divide, which is a ridge running from South to North. All the streams to the West of it, empty into the Pacific Ocean, and all streams to the East of it, empty into the Atlantic Ocean; including the Gulf of Mexico.

3. *"... yet the sea is not full ..."* to overflowing, as the rivers sometimes are. WHY? The sun draws water from the ocean by evaporation. Then there are the "Waterspouts" mentioned in *Psa. 42:7.*

16

4. The "waterspout" is a means that God uses to siphon water from the earth and suspends it in the clouds; then returns it to the earth in rain or snow. I have seen waterspouts, many times in the Pacific. It is an awesome sight, to see the wind whirling the water in a circle that becomes a conduit, sucking the water upward.

The lesson here is that man is never satisfied, always restless, never contented. The more he has of the world, the more he wants of the world. As Peter said in II Pet. 3:4b, "... *all things continue as they were from the beginning of the creation.*"

V-8.   "*All things are full of labour; man cannot utter it:*" (or change it).

Because God pronounced this penalty upon man in *Gen. 3:17-19* "*the eye is not satisfied with seeing, ...*" We see a beautiful new sight that holds our attention for awhile, and then we ignore it, and look for something new to adore. This is the "lust of the eyes" that John speaks of in *I John 2:16.*

1. Jesus warns against this in *Matt. 13:13-16* and again in *Mark 4:12.*

2. Our eyes need to be anointed, as seen in *Rev. 3:18,* for one day we shall look upon Jesus according to *Rev. 1:7.* "*... nor the ear filled with hearing.*" We may hear a beautiful tune, or phrase, or poem; but we soon forget them. Our curiosity carries us on to hear something new.

V-9.   "*The thing that hath been, it is that which shall be ...*"

Sound confusing? It simply means that mans curiosity which causes him to invent new things, and explore new horizons in the past, will be the same drive that will keep him doing them in the future. Man always wants something bigger, better, faster, more stylish, but he is never satisfied with what he has. Paul could say something that not many christians can say. In *Phil. 4:11* he says, "*Not that I speak in respect of want: for I have learned, that in whatsoever state I am, therewith to be content."* This was a lesson he had to learn. *I Tim. 6:6-7-* *"But godliness with contentment is GREAT GAIN."* Verse 7, *"For we brought nothing into this world, and it is CERTAIN we can carry nothing out."* There is no reason to pack a suitcase in preparation for dying.

Psa. 106:29 warns us, *"Thus they provoke him to anger with their inventions: and the plague brake in upon them."*

Prov. 8:12 tells us, *"I wisdom dwell with prudence, and find out knowledge of witty inventions."*

"... and there is no new thing under the sun."

That God doesn't know about, or that is hidden from Him, that is.

Verse nine tells us, "There is no new thing under the sun." Verse 10 is re-affirming that statement. I believe the Preacher is comparing God, the Omniscient One, with man and his limited knowledge. For instance, the latest news, to me, is old news to someone else, and still older news to God, who knows all things from beginning to end. Therefore there are no surprises with God.

V-10.   Think of all the inventions of man since Adam and Eve. Man thinks every time he comes up with another invention, that it is something never before thought of.

But where did he get the knowledge and the wisdom to put it all together?

1.   Solomon is known for his wisdom. In fact, in *I Kings 10:24* the scripture declares, "And all the earth sought to Solomon, to hear his wisdom, *which God had put in his heart*." So, whose wisdom was it?? READ *I Kings 3:12; 4:29* and *5:12* to find out whose wisdom he had.

2.   *"... it hath been already of old time, which was before us."* Who is writing this? Solomon. He knew that what wisdom he possessed it had already, of old, been in the mind of God.

18

3. If every person, who invents something they think is NEW, would just give God the glory, and recognize the fact that God knew all about it long before they had the first thought on the subject; there would be no limit to what God would allow man to accomplish.

V-11. *"There is no remembrance of former things ... "*

One generation forgets what former generations have done for civilization, and yet, advancement in the technology of 3,000 years ago, was just as important to that generation as ours is to we who live in this modern generation.

1. Yet for all of our modern inventions, the truth is that: *"... neither shall there be any remembrance of things that are to come, with those that shall come after."*

2. Think of this! IF Christ does not come for another thousand years, those who are living at that time will have forgotten, and far surpassed, all of our modern conveniences of today. See *Eccl. 2:16,* and *9:5.*

3. To sum up the last two verses, we conclude that all life for man (apart from God) lies in the present. The past has come and gone, it is over and done with. The future for the unregenerate man is VERY uncertain.

4. BUT, for the child of God, we may not know what the future holds, but thank God, we know WHO holds the future. May we be able to say with Paul in *II Tim. 1:12,* "For the which cause I also suffer these things: nevertheless I am not ashamed: for I know whom I have believed, and am persuaded that he is able to keep that which I have committed unto him against that day."

V-12. *"I the Preacher was king over Israel in Jerusalem."*

And, as king, Solomon had opportunity to view all classes of people under him, from the richest to the poorest. He had access to every matter in his kingdom. He had the greatest minds of that day, at his disposal. Therefore he had first hand knowledge, and is speaking from experience.

In verses 12-18 we find man striving for wisdom, apart from God, and the extremes he will go to, to get it. Man has the mistaken idea that wisdom comes through education; but this is folly. Wisdom comes from God, according to *I Kings 4:29*, "God gave Solomon wisdom and understanding exceeding much." Listen to *Job 28:12*, "But where shall wisdom be found? and where is the place of understanding?" V-13, "Man knoweth not the price thereof; neither is it found in the land of the living." READ *Job 14-28*.

V-12   (cont.) "*I the Preacher was king over Israel in Jerusalem.*"

He was anointed by Nathan and acknowledged as King, at the age of 19 or 20, in the year 1015 B.C.

1. Here in Ecclesiastes, he is telling of his past experiences while he was king. History tells us he died while he was still king. he reigned forty years, and died as an old man at age 60.

2. Solomon wrote Proverbs and Song of Solomon while he was still young, and this book when he was older and experienced with life.

3. There is a lesson here for us. Regardless of Solomon's wisdom, it did not teach him self-control. There is no record of this man ever repenting of his sins, as his father David did in *Psa. 51*.

4. Read *Neh. 13:26*; and *I Kings 11:1-7*. It seems from reading *Eccl. 2:17* that he was wearied with life.

V-13.   He put his whole heart into finding out by experience, "*All things that are done under heaven ...*"

1. If true joy and satisfaction could be found in worldly pleasure, Solomon would have found it.

2. It seems that Solomon participated in every thing known to man, not for his own pleasure only, but so that he could instruct and direct future generations away from the vanity of the world.

3. "*... this sore travail hath God given to the sons of man to be exercised therewith.*" Travail means physical or mental exertion, agony, or torment. *Eccl.*

20

2:23, 26. Man feels compelled to exercise all of these things in order to understand himself and God.

V-14. "*I have seen all the works that are done under the sun;*"

    1. Solomon has seen man agonizing and striving for wisdom and knowledge apart from God, and here is the result of his finding: "*... and behold, all is vanity and vexation of the spirit.*"

    2. In *Hosea 12:1* it is said of Ephraim, "Ephraim feedeth on wind." *Isa. 44:20* tells us, "He (man) feedeth on ashes: a deceived heart hath turned him aside, that he cannot deliver his soul, nor say is there not a lie in my right hand." See *Eccl. 2:11, 17, 26.*

V-15. This verse is a confirmation of V-14.

    "*That which is crooked cannot be made straight:*"

    That is, by man himself. This is because of the corrupt nature that we were born with, which we learn, from such passages as *Jer. 17:9; Isa. 1:5-6;* and *Eccl. 7:13.*

    "*... and that which is wanting cannot be numbered.*"

    The meaning of this phrase is simply that our wants are never ending, and far to numerous to count. The last part of *Jer. 44:18* says, "We have wanted all things, and have been consumed by the sword and by the famine." Sword and famine are the end result of wanting to many of the wrong things, such as riches, drugs, and pleasures.

There is an interesting passage of scripture in *Job 15:1-13.* Here Eliphaze is chiding Job for letting his mouth condemn him. He said in V-6, "Thine own mouth condemneth thee." Job says in *Job 9:20* that his own mouth would condemn him. How many times has our thoughts condemned us, for something our mouth said. In this respect, we should pray the prayer that David prayed in *Psa. 141:3.* He prayed, "Set a watch, O Lord, before my mouth; keep the door of my lips."

V-16. Here, the preacher has communed with his own heart. It is beneficial for us to take an unbiased, self-searching look at our own heart. *I John 3:20-21.*

1. Refusing to do so could bring the chastening of God upon us. *Deut. 8:5*, "Thou shalt also consider in thine heart, that, as a man chasteneth his son, so the Lord thy God chasteneth thee."

2. *Psa. 4:4*, "Stand in awe, and sin not; commune with your own heart upon your bed, and be still."

3. *Psa. 77:6*, "I call to remembrance my song in the night: I commune with mine own heart: and my spirit made diligent search." It simply means, we must communicate, and keep in touch with self.

4. *"Lo I am come to great estate,"* He was a man of great social standing and rank and had great wealth. He belonged to what we call the upper class of society. *I Kings 3:12,13. "... and have gotten more wisdom that all they that have been before me in Jerusalem."* He is remembering what God told him in *I Kings 3:12.*

   "... my heart had great experience of wisdom and knowledge." He learned much from his own heart. *Prov. 14:10* says, "The heart knoweth his own bitterness." *Prov. 16:9* says, "A mans heart deviseth his way: but the Lord directeth his steps." *Prov. 19:21* tells us, "There are many devices in a mans heart; nevertheless the counsel of the Lord, that shall stand." We find our Lords teaching on the heart in *Matt. 15:18-19*, and *Matt. 12:35.*

V-17. *"And I gave my heart to know wisdom, and to know madness and folly;"* Folly means foolishness.

1. Solomon not only had the power and benefit of knowledge, but he also experienced the amusement and entertainment of it.

2. He digested all of these things and knew how to make use of them, in warning you and me of their consequences.

3. Listen to *Prov. 2:10-11*, It seems that God is equipping Solomon for the purpose stated in *Prov. 22:21.*

22

Solomon is saying, I gave my heart to the rules and instructions of wisdom.

4. "... *and to know madness and folly:*" That I might warn, and possibly prevent others from falling under its influence.

5. "... *I perceive that this also is vexation of the spirit.*" This was the final result of all his experiences. His searches were very tiring, to both mind and spirit. *V. 13.* (sore travail).

V-18. He found that the mixing of wisdom and folly (foolishness) was vexing to his spirit and peace of mind.

A. It grieved him to see those with wisdom, not use it.

B. And those who knew folly, not resisting it, but continuing in it.

1. *"For in much wisdom is much grief:"* All of the philosophy and politics in the world, cannot restore the old fleshly nature of man.

2. Men go to great extremes to get wisdom and knowledge, but the more they get the more they want, and the more they realize how much more there is out there, to learn. It grieves man that he still doesn't have all the answers, in his search, for past blunders and mistakes.

3. *"... and he that increaseth knowledge increaseth sorrow."* How is this so? Because they have a greater perception of the calamities that await the world. Jesus said in *Luke 12:48,* "For unto whomsoever much is given, of him shall much be required; and to whom have committed much, of him they will ask the more."

4. *II Tim. 3:7* puts it all in perspective, when the Apostle Paul said, "Ever learning, and NEVER able to come to the knowledge of the truth."

Chapter 2

In chapter one we have the introduction of VANITY, in verses 1-3. In verses 4-11, we see the illustrations of vanity, while in verses 12-18 we see the vanity of striving after wisdom (apart from God). Here in chapter two, we see the striving after pleasure. We live in a pleasure mad world today, and pleasure is a multi-billion dollar industry in America, let alone the rest of the world.

V-1. *"I said in mine heart, Go to now, I will prove thee with mirth;"*

This was a deliberate project with the preacher. He sets out to convince himself that having fun(mirth), will make him happy. We know that the term "heart", in the bible, means mind, brain, and heart, and is the seat of our emotions and affections.

"... therefore enjoy pleasure ...:"

Pleasure is an interesting word. Mr. Webster says it means, "A state of gratification." This includes "sensual gratification"(lust of the flesh). The word also means, "frivolous amusement", and a source of delight or joy. Different people find pleasure in different things, depending upon their relationship with God.

1. The unsaved find pleasure in sensual gratification only. The lust of the eyes, the lust of the flesh, and the pride of life, is all that motivates them. But listen to Paul in *I Tim. 5:6,* "But she that liveth to pleasure is dead (spiritually) while she liveth."

2. We have the parable of the rich fool, in *Luke 12:16-21.* This young man had *I* trouble, and it culminated in *V-19.* But in the very next verse, Jesus calls this man a fool, and this attitude cost him his life. James warns the rich in *James 5:5.*

25

3. CHRISTIANS find pleasure and deep abiding joy, in those things that please God. *Psa. 111:2*, "The works of the Lord are great, sought out of all them that have pleasure therein." (that is, in the works of God). A. In *Psa. 16:11*, David found pleasure in the *presence of the Lord.* He said, "Thou wilt show me the path of life: in thy presence is fullness of joy; at thy right hand there are pleasures for evermore." Read *Job 36:10-11*. It may be that our ears have never been opened to discipline.

4. God is NOT opposed to pleasure for His children, but He means for us to find that pleasure in Him, as opposed to the world. We learn from *Psa. 36:8* that He has RIVERS of pleasures for His children.

V-2. He (the preacher) has reached a sad conclusion to the matter of striving after pleasure, apart from God.

1. Laughing at the WRONG things, is folly to God. In this respect, he said in *Eccl. 7:3,* "Sorrow is better than laughter:for by the sadness of the countenance the heart is made better." *V-6* says, "For as the crackling of thorns under a pot, so is the laughter of the fool: this also is vanity."

2. "... *of mirth, What doeth it?*" Or, what does it accomplish that is lasting and beneficial to the soul?

3. *Isa. 24:5-11* predicts a day, when all mirth and laughter will be taken from the earth. This is during the great tribulation period when there will be no merriment for mankind.

We have this great man, experimenting in just about every area of life, pertaining to the flesh. He has shown us the vanity of striving after wisdom and pleasure, apart from God; and the emptiness of it all. He comes to the conclusion, that life is absolutely meaningless, when lived for the flesh only, with no hope for eternity. Our Lord, Himself, asked this question in *Matt. 16:26,* "For what is a man profited, if he shall gain the whole

26

world, and lose his own soul? or what shall a man give in exchange for his soul?

V-3. *"I sought in mine heart to give myself unto wine, yet acquainting mine heart with wisdom;"*

1. He is exploring another avenue of worldly pleasure, and one in which much sin and iniquity is found.

   Prov. 20:1 tells us, "Wine is a *mocker* strong drink is raging: and whosoever is deceived thereby is not wise." Noah, a great man of God, is an example of the deception and mockery of wine, when used in excess. *Gen. 9:20-24.* It brought a lifetime of servitude upon one of his sons. *V. 25-27.*

2. The preacher planned to use wisdom in this experiment; but had forgotten his own advice in *Prov. 20,* that strong drink is deceptive. It has a way of taking control of the imbiber. If every drunk could see themselves, while in this condition, it would have a profound effect on them.

3. In this verse, he reveals the reason for his experimenting in these different areas of life. "... *and to lay hold of folly (foolish actions or conduct) til I might see what was that good for the sons of men, which they should do under heaven all the days of their life."*

4. I believe God the Father allowed Solomon to indulge in all of these pursuits, knowing that he would tell us the truth and instruct us, that we might escape the consequences of their entrapment.

V-4-8. We group these verses together because they all explain the same great truth; the vanity of "great works" or accomplishments.

1. "... *I builded me houses ..."* It is said that Solomons Temple was one of the wonders of the world.

2. His personal dwelling took 13 years to build, according to *I Kings 7:1.* It was 150 feet long, 75 feet wide, and 45 feet high. That amounts to 11,250

27

square feet for one story. It was 45 feet high, and could have been several stories.

3.   He spent 20 years building the Temple and the kings house. *I Kings 9:10*. The construction of the Temple is found in *I Kings* 6:1-38.

V-5.   *"I made me gardens and orchards,..."* His gardens were the most beautiful in all the world. My wife would have been raptured, if she could have seen his gardens.

V-6.   *"I made me pools of water, ..."* No doubt for irrigation.

1.   He is said to have built an aqueduct from Etham to Jerusalem. This is a canal engineered to keep water flowing gently, over long distances.

2.   History tells us, he built 3 pools of enormous size. One was 582 ft. deep. That is a deep hole in the ground. The second pool was 432'x250'x39' deep. The third was 380'x236'x25' deep. They were constructed in such a way that they drained into each other.

3   Solomon was wise enough to control himself in all of these pursuits, but many are not, and should take heed to these scriptures.

We are still in the section of scriptures, dealing with the vanity of material possessions and personal accomplishments. *Vs. 4-17.* In all of Solomon's "great" works, he still maintained his integrity and wisdom. We learn from Solomon that not all GREAT works are GOOD works. They may be great in mans sight and disallowed by God. Jesus said in *Matt. 23:5,* concerning the scribes and Pharisees, "But all their works they do for to be seen of men."

V-7.   *"I got me servants and maidens, and had servants born in my house;"*

We can readily understand that with everything Solomon had going for him, it would take a vast amount of help and organization, to keep it all together.

For instance, concerning the servants born in the house, *Ezra 2:58* tells us the children of Solomons servants numbered 292. Besides that, he had 700 wives and 300 concubines. *I Kings 11:3.*

I Kings 4:26 says, "And Solomon had 40,000 stalls of horses for his chariots, and 12,000 horsemen, to take care of 40,000 horses.

"*... also I had great possessions of great and small cattle ...*"

The word "cattle" here in V-7 has a different meaning than the word we use today. We think of cattle as meaning bulls, cows, and steers, but we use the word "stock" as meaning all the animals on the farm; which is the meaning of the word "cattle", here in our text. The words "great" and "small" probably mean oxen and sheep, of which Solomon had plenty. We are told in *I Kings 8:36* that he made a peace offering unto the Lord, of 22,000 oxen and 120,000 sheep. That ought to have brought him a lot of peace. *I Kings 4:22-23* gives a list of partial provisions for one day, just for his household.

V-8. "*I gathered me also silver and gold, and the peculiar treasure of kings*"

Treasures that only kings usually have. I have seen the "crown jewels" in London, as well as the art work in two palaces; yet these would not compare to Solomons wealth. Read *I Kings 10:14-27*. A talent of gold weighs 229 1/6 lb. (troy wt.) which is 12oz. to the pound. This would amount to almost 76 tons of gold, and about $3.83 billion income per year.

"*I gat me men singers and women singers,*" There is no doubt, he had the very best in the world, at his command, along with the very best instruments that money could buy.

V-9. "*So I was great, and increased more than all that were before me in Jerusalem;*"

Solomon is not boasting here, he is stating a fact backed up by scripture. *II Chron. 9:22* tells us, "And

King Solomon passed all the kings of the earth in riches and wisdom." Read *I Kings 3:5-13.*

"... *also my wisdom remained with me."*

He kept his integrity intact through these times of prosperity, for the purpose mentioned in V-3, "Til I might see what was that good for the sons of men." He kept the purpose of his pursuit in mind, and exercised self restraint, which many christians are unable to do.

V-10.   Solomon experienced every avenue of worldly pleasure, expressed in *I John 2:16-17.*

    (1) The lust of the flesh.

    (2) The lust of the eyes.

    (3) The pride of life.

    However, John said this is not of the Father, but is of the world. Our Lord warns us of these things in *Matt. 6:2; Luke l6:25. See Eccl. 6:2.*

We are still on the subject of the VANITY of personal works or great accomplishments. Our Lord warns against the "god of mammon" in *Matt. 6:24,* when he said, "No man can serve two masters: for either he will hate the one, and love the other; or else he will hold to the one and despise the other. Ye cannot serve God and mammon." (material wealth). Then in *Matt. 19:24* we find the controversial subject of the camel and the needle. Jesus said, "Again I say unto you, it is easier for the camel to go through the eye of a needle, than for a rich man to enter the kingdom of God."

V-11.   The preacher now looks back upon the things he had accomplished in verses 1-10. He concluded that none of them contributed any lasting benefit for man, spiritually.

    1.   He had made an earnest inquiry in *Eccl. 1:3.* He asked the question, "What profit hath a man of all his labour which he taketh under the sun."

    2.   Here in V-11, he uses the word "profit" again, and says there is no profit in material wealth. That is, for eternity. It will not benefit us in the after-life.

3. In *Eccl. 6:2* it may even become an evil disease. Covetousness and greed are contagious.

V-12. In *Eccl. 1:17* Solomon sets out to experiment in three things: *wisdom, madness* (rage,ecstacy, and enthusiasm) and folly (foolishness, meaningless, trivial behavior).

1. Now here in V-12, he is looking back upon these pursuits (I turned myself to behold) and weighing them, individually, to assess their value.

2. Do we ever take this kind of inventory of our ACTIONS and HABITS? They may become madness and folly, if we do not keep a close watch upon them. *Heb. 2:1,* "Therefore we ought to give the more earnest heed to the things which we have heard, lest at any time we should let them slip." (or drift away).

"... *for what can the man do that cometh after the king?*" Solomon had all the WEALTH he wanted, all the TIME he wanted, all the OPPORTUNITY he needed, so who could possibly explore more of these experiments than Solomon?

1. That being a fact, why don't more professed christians take warning from this wise man? Notice the next sentence here in V-12, "...*even that which hath already been done.*"

2. ALL any man, who followed him, could do, would NOT give more insight in the consequences of a life of pleasure.

3. No doubt he would lack the self control and the ability to maintain his integrity as Solomon did, and would suffer greater consequences than Solomon did. Even Solomon went to far, and displeased the Lord. Read *I Kings 11:1-11.*

V-13. "*Then I saw that wisdom excelleth folly, as far as light excelleth darkness.*" Of the three, wisdom,madness and folly; wisdom won out. (1) In *Eccl. 7:12* WISDOM is a defense. (2) WISDOM giveth life to them that have it.

It is wisdom that gives the true meaning to all other pursuits, and helps us to keep a proper perspective on life in general. The contrast between wisdom and folly is like contrasting light and darkness.

1. We are warned in *Isa. 5:20* about being unable to distinguish the difference between things of darkness(worldly) and things of light(spiritual).

    Jesus tells us in *John 3:19* that darkness brings condemnation upon those who walk therein. "And this is the condemnation, that light is come into the world, and men loved darkness rather than light, because their deeds were evil." BUT wisdom lets us tell the difference.

Solomon has been experimenting with various pursuits to find something lasting and beneficial to the soul, but comes to realize their futility when compared to eternity. WISDOM was one of his greatest discoveries. Apart from God, man's wisdom is foolishness with God. *I Cor. 1:18-21 and 26-31.*

V-14. *"The wise man's eyes are in his head;"* You may say, isn't that where everyone's eyes are? Physically speaking, yes, but the unwise do not use their head. They do not think about what they see, in terms of how God sees that same thing. This is what Jesus meant in *Mark 8:18* when He said, "having eyes, ye see not." David said the same thing in *Psa. 115:5-7. "but the fool walketh in darkness:"* His eyes might as well be in the BACK of his head. This is spiritual darkness. *Psa. 14:1* says, "The fool hath said in his heart, there is no God. They are corrupt, they have done abominable works, there is none that doeth good,"

1. Jesus said in *I John 12:35,* "Yet a little while is the light with you. Walk while ye have light lest darkness come upon you: for he that walketh in darkness(spiritual) knoweth not whither he goeth."

2. In Solomon's wisdom, he perceived (understood) that there was one event that happened to all, wise or foolish.

3.   That one event is death, which equalizes all of society.

4.   Death is no respecter of persons. *Heb. 9:27,* "It is appointed unto man once to die, and after this the judgement." From this passage, we learn: Where death finds us, eternity will keep us.

V-15.   Solomon, in all his wisdom, riches, experiments, could not escape death, any more than the fool.

"*... and why was I then more wise?* What did his short lived superiority accomplish?

1. Is the world affected by Solomon's wisdom and exploits? NO! Even christians are not overly impressed with his teaching.

2. There is one great exception to this overpowering enemy, called death. *Prov. 14:32,* "The wicked is driven away in his wickedness: (from God) but the righteous hath hope in his death." This present life, for the christian, is just a training ground for eternity.

3. Isaiah had this hope of another life, when he said in *Isa. 25:8,* "He will swallow up death in victory; and the Lord God will wipe away tears from off ALL faces; and the rebuke of his people shall he take away from off all the earth for the Lord God hath spoken it."

V-16.   "*For there is no remembrance of the wise more than the fool forever.*"

ILLUSTRATION: The tower of Babel in *Gen. 11:4.* It was to be built to exalt man and his wisdom, but do you think the world ever thinks about that failed project? If they did think about it, would they learn anything from it?

1.   Man wants to build monuments to himself, but they do not impress God.

2.   On the other end of the spectrum of humanity, are the sons of God made righteous through the shed blood of Jesus Christ, who are held in everlasting remembrance by our God. *Psa. 112:6* and *Heb. 6:10.*

3. What ever is accomplished in this present day will also be forgotten, in time, by future generations. *"And how dieth the wise man? as the fool."* His wisdom does not protect him from death, but it can help him prepare for the after-life; which will take the STING out of dying, as we are told in *I Cor. 15:54-57.*

In our last lesson we learned that wisdom does not protect a person from death, but it can help prepare for the AFTER life, and can take the STING out of death, for the saved person. The christian who has made any advancement in wisdom and knowledge of scripture, has no fear of death. *I Cor. 15:55-57.*

V-17. The preacher ends the discourse on the vanity of great accomplishments with this observation:
"THEREFORE I HATED LIFE;"

1. In every experiment he has tried, he has been disappointed to the extent that he is weary of life.
2. This is the end result of living for the flesh, and this life only. As Paul said in *I Cor. 15:19,* "If in this life only we have hope in Christ, we are of all men most miserable." Then Job tells us in *Job 16:2* that "THINGS (possessions) ARE MISERABLE COMFORTERS."
"... because the work that is wrought under the sun is grievous to me:"
1. It has no lasting benefit and will come back to haunt him.
2. We may be like the church of Laodicea, in *Rev. 3:17,* "Rich and increased with goods, and have need of nothing." But they had a greater need than they realized.
3. Solomon probably felt this way, many times during his life, because of his great riches and wisdom. Here in these verses he has taken a good look at the conclusion of the matter. SEE *Eccl. 12:13.*

V-18.   In the next few verses (18-23) we see the vanity of hard labour. *"Yea, I hated all my labour which I had taken under the sun."*

    1.   Would he have felt the same way, had he dispensed his wealth to help the poor while he was living, and could see the enjoyment it brought to others.

    2.   *Psa. 112:5,* "A good man sheweth favour and lendeth: he will guide his affairs with discretion."

    3.   *Prov. 19:17,* "He that hath pity upon the poor lendeth unto the Lord; and that which he hath given will he pay him again."

"because I should leave it unto the man that shall be after me."

    1. Wealth seems to give a false sense of security. *Psa. 49:10-11. Verse 11* says, "Their inward thought is that their houses shall continue forever."

V-19.   *"And who knoweth whether he shall be a wise man or a fool?"*

    1.   Therefore it would seem to be much wiser to use wealth while you are living, that you may have a certain amount of control over it. Read *Psa. 112:1-9.*

    2.   His wisdom, wealth, and hard work has accomplished nothing good, if a fool has control over it at the wise man's death. These are practical lessons, for the use of wealth. Read *Psa. 39:5-6.*

    3.   Scripture tells us that Rehoboam, Solomon's son by an idolatrous woman of the Ammonites, named Naamah, followed Solomon as king. See *I* Kings 14:21. *Verse 22* tells us that Judah did evil in the sight of the Lord. It sounds like the parable of the rich young fool in *Luke 12:16-21.*

V-20.   Solomon seems to have despaired of life in general, which is the natural consequences of living "life under the sun", or for worldly pursuits only.

1. I believe this is what we call healthful bitterness. It causes us to take a good look at our motives and actions.
2. Like the rich young fool in Luke, God told the Israelites that they would, "Plant vineyards, and dress them, but shall neither drink of the wine, nor gather the grapes; for the worms shall eat them." *Deut. 28:39.*
3. Solomon is no longer enjoying the things he set out to experiment with.

I believe what the preacher means in V-20, is that he turned from hard work(labour) to despair, for all the efforts he had expended, under the sun. This is a continuation of the vanity of hard labour. The reason for his despair is that he now realizes that others will have an opportunity to squander all that he had laboured to obtain, and that the person might even be a fool.

V-21. Many who have obtained great wealth, have done so by three methods: WISDOM, KNOWLEDGE, EQUITY (or skill). If he has to leave his wealth to a man "*that hath not laboured therein*" or who has done absolutely nothing to earn this sudden wealth, it is "*VANITY AND A GREAT EVIL.*" WHY? For two reasons:
1. Because the wise man that gained the wealth, should have put it to better use. Instead of hoarding it, spread it around to help others. Read *Prov. 10:15-16.* God warned His people in *Deut. 8:17-19* about wealth. In *Job 21:13,* God told Job, "They spend their days in great wealth, and in a moment go down to the grave." Read *Prov. 13:11* and *20:21.*
2. Because the person receiving the inheritance, many times, will not appreciate it, nor use it wisely. In that case, all the wealth accumulated by the wise, brings no lasting benefit to anyone. He will have a lot of friends, while his money lasts, but when it is gone, so are his friends. *Prov. 19:4* tells us, "Wealth maketh many friends, but the poor is separated from his neighbor.

V-22. and V-23. *"For what hath a man of all his labour,"* In *Ch. 1:3,* we find the word *PROFIT*, connected with this question. *PROFIT* is what we have left, after everything else is paid for. In other words, what have we laid up for eternity, after a life time of hard work? What kind of material have we sent on ahead of us, that will bring rewards at the Judgement Seat of Christ? *I Cor. 3:9-15* and *II Cor. 5:1, 10.* The bottom line is, why should we spend endless days and sleepless nights, acquiring this worlds goods, if this is the end of it? We need to heed our Lord's warning in *Luke 12:15,* "And he said unto them, Take heed,and beware of covetousness: for a mans life consisteth not in the abundance of things which he possesseth." I believe we could truly say a man's character will be determined by the things which possess the man. In the verses following *Luke 12:15,* our Lord gives the parable of the rich fool.

V-24. It seems that after all the gloom and despair, a light comes on suddenly for the preacher and he has a flash of inspiration. He has now found the KEY: happiness and true joy, from a life of labour. There is nothing wrong with enjoying the fruits of our labour, as long as we stay focused on the main objective for life. Here is the key, *"And that he should make his SOUL enjoy good in his labour."* The SOUL is eternal, and he has done something that will last for eternity(with his wealth).

Paul told young Timothy in *I Tim. 6:6,* "But godliness with contentment is great gain." *V-7,* "For we brought nothing into this world, and it is certain we can carry nothing out." Read *Phil. 4:11- 13.* We need peace, regardless of circumstances. *"This also I saw, that it was from the hand of God."* We learn from this passage that God is the source of all lasting joy and benefit from all our works here on earth, a we live a life of obedience to His divine will.

The second chapter concludes with the exhortation to be content, or satisfied, as *Heb. 13:5* puts it, "Let your conversation be without covetousness; and be content with such things as ye have: for he hath said, I will never leave thee, not forsake thee." (that alone,ought to make us content) Paul told Timothy in *I Tim. 6:8,* "And having food and raiment let us be therewith content." He said in V-6, "But godliness with contentment is great gain." The key word here is "godliness" or God-likeness.

V-25.   *"For who can eat or who else can hasten hereunto more than I?"*

      1.   The meaning seems to be, who can compete with me, in the pursuit of all these things, previously mentioned? IF Solomon, with all his wealth and opportunities, failed to find enjoyment, who else can?

      2.   I sometimes think that God denies His people (or some of them) wealth and riches, to spare them the heartbreak and misery that worldly possessions bring upon them.

      3.   This is also the reason God gives us the benefit of Solomon's experiences, that we might not have to pay the price that he paid.

V-26.   *"For God giveth to man that is good in his sight, wisdom, and knowledge, and joy:"*

      Prov. 13:22. "A good man leaveth an inheritance to his children's children: and the wealth of the sinner is laid up for the just." God gives His children wisdom and knowledge to enjoy what they have. *Psa. 84:11* tells us, "For the Lord God is a sun and shield:the Lord will give grace and glory: *no good thing will he withhold from them that walk uprightly.*" And then in the beatitudes of *Matt. 5:5* Jesus said, "Blessed are the meek for *they shall inherit the earth.*"

      "... but to the sinner he giveth travail,"

      1.   This is mental torture and anguish, as well as physical toil and hard labour. The sinner does not have the wisdom of God, to know how to distribute his

wealth, that his SOUL (V-24) might enjoy it. *He is not thinking of his soul.*

2. The godly Solomon had satisfaction and joy in his wealth, when God first gave them to him in *II Chron. l:1-12.*

3. However the backslidden Solomon found no pleasure in them, when he parted ways with the Lord, (or apart from God).We are told in *II Chron. 12:9* that his wealth ended up in the hands of a man by the name of Shishak king of Egypt.

4. We know that God can distribute (or redistribute) any or all of the wealth in the universe as he sees fit. For He is the Sovereign of all creation. Read *Psa. 50:10-12; Job 41:11; Deut. 10:14 and Matt. 25:28.*

"This also ..." This gathering and heaping up goods, by sinners without enjoying them, is "... *vanity and vexation of the spirit."*

Chapter 3

We readily understand that God determines the course of nature, from reading *Eccl. 1:5-7,* but do we understand that God also determines the events of this life? Everything works according to cycles and seasons, including human beings; yet man is the only part of God's creation that abuses his privileges, here on earth. In fact, we are warned about this abuse in *I Cor. 7:31.*

V-1. *"To every thing there is a season,"*

1. There is a time or season of suffering, but it makes us stronger christians. *II Tim. 2:12* tells us, "If we suffer, we shall also reign with him: if we deny him he also will deny us."

2. Paul had many seasons of suffering, just as our Lord told him he would, in *Acts 9:16,* "For I will show him how great things he must suffer for my name's sake."

3. There are also seasons of REJOICING, and in *Acts 5:41* suffering and rejoicing are united in the Apostles. We read, "And they departed from the presence of the council, rejoicing that they were counted worthy to *suffer shame* for his name."

4. In *Phil. 4:4* Paul said, "Rejoice in the Lord alway: again I say rejoice."

5. In *Luke 10:20b* Jesus said, "Rejoice because your names are written in heaven."

"... and a time to every purpose under heaven."

This word "purpose" means, INTENTION, RESOLUTION, or DETERMINATION. We know that God works on his own schedule, not man's.

1. *Prov. 20:18,* "Every PURPOSE is established by counsel (Godhead) and with advice make war." (or carry out the purpose).

41

V-2.   "*A time to be born, a time to die:*"

       1. The gestation period (from conception to birth) of a human is 9 months, and that baby is going to be born whether anyone else is ready or not, because God said it was time for the birth to happen. A TIME TO BE BORN.

       2. I also believe that every person born, has a certain amount of time allotted to them, and that time is determined by God. In *Job 14:1* we read, "Man that is born of woman is of few days, and full of trouble." V-5 says, "Seeing his days are determined, the number of his months are with thee,(God) thou hast appointed his bounds that he cannot pass." (Or extend the boundary lines).

       3. *Heb. 9:27,* "It is appointed unto man once to die, and after this the judgement."

       4. We also know that God can add to those days or months, if He sees fit.

       5. We have an example of this in *II Kings 20:1-6.*

"*... a time to plant, and a time to pluck up that which is planted;*"

       1. The farmer must understand and remember the seasons for planting and harvesting his crops. He dare not deviate very far from those times.

       2. The seasons are controlled by the moon, and man has absolutely no control over that part of creation.

          A. *Gen. 1:14,* "And God said, let there be lights in the firmament of the heaven to divide the day from the night; and let them be for signs, and for *seasons,* and for days and years."

          B. *Psa. 104:19,* "He appointed the moon for seasons: the sun knoweth his going down."

       3. The farmer must also harvest his crops at the right time, for there is a time to PLUCK UP.

       4. This verse may also apply to the death and resurrection of the believer.

5. In death we are planted, and in the resurrection we are plucked up. Paul explains this process in *I Cor. 15:35-58.*

In determining the events of life for man, God's plan and timing is sometimes far different than ours may be. Jesus told his apostles in *Acts 1:7*, "It is NOT for you to know the *times* or *seasons*, which the Father hath put in his own power." When we stop to think about it, we admit that God's way, and God's time is always best even though we may not agree at the time we ask for something from him. It might help if we remember what God told Isaiah in chapter *55:8-11.* Let's explore a little more of this mine field of truth, with the preacher Solomon.

V-3.   "*A time to kill*" WHAT? BY WHOM?
1. We find part of the answer in *Acts 10:9-15*, where Peter had his vision of the great sheet let down from heaven. *V-10* tells us Peter was "VERY HUNGRY" and in *V-13* God told him to, "Kill and eat."
2. Human beings killing each other is NOT what is meant here, even though man taking another mans life, *in judgement*, is scriptural, according to *Gen. 9:6*, where capital punishment is sanctioned.
3. "*A time to kill*" may also refer to the time of judgement upon the earth when God will do the killing, spoken of in *Rev. 6:8,* during the opening of the fourth seal.
4. God absolutely condemns the senseless taking of another life. Read *Hos. 4:1-2.*

"... *a time to heal*". WHAT? There is physical and spiritual healing.
1. We find the word "heal" used for the first time in scripture by Moses in *Num. 12:10-13.* It concerned his sister, Miriam, whom God had turned leprous. This was physical healing needed here.
2. We know that Christ gave his Apostles power to heal all manner of sickness and disease in *Matt.*

43

10:1 and 8. JESUS HIMSELF performed many miracles of healing. Matt. 4:23.

3. There is also SPIRITUAL healing, found in the Bible.This is what God promised his people in *II Chron. 7:14.* This is also what David prayed for in *Psa. 41:4* when he prayed, "Lord, be merciful unto me: *heal my soul:* I have sinned against thee."

4. In *Hos. 14:4* where God said to Israel, "I will heal their backsliding, I will love them freely: for mine anger is turned away from him."

"... a time to break down," WHAT?

1. Break down the walls of sin that Satan tries to build around us. *Psa. 2:8,9,* and *Isa. 5:5.*

2. There is coming a day when God will break the chains of sin, forever. We find a type of this in *Jer. 31:28.*

3. We are told in *Ezek. 26:4, 12* that God will break down the walls of untempered mortar, that man has built around himself. *Psa. 72:4.*

"... a time to build up."

1. There was a set time for Christ to come to the earth and build his church. *Matt. 16:18* gives the time and place that this fact took place.

2. We are to be builders of walls of protection for our children and each other. *Isa. 58:11,12.*

3. The word of God and his grace, builds up the christian for service. Acts 20:32.

4. There is a time to build upon the foundation of our salvation, but we are warned about building with the wrong materials in *I Cor. 3:10-11.*

We are still in the section dealing with the events of life. We believe that God pre-determines these events, and that they apply to ALL men(or to all the human race). BUT I think we could also say that the teaching, here in Ecclesiastes, only makes sense to those who are spiritually minded,that Paul is talking about in *I Cor. 2:15-16,* "He that is spiritual judgeth ALL things."

V-4. *"A time to weep,"*

1. There are many reasons for shedding tears, in the Bible.
2. Like everything else, there is a difference between God and man as to what we are to weep over.

   A *Jer. 22:10* tells us we are not to weep over the dead, but we are told to weep over the backslider or, "He that goeth away." (from God).

   B. We are encouraged to weep over lost souls. In *Psa. 126:5-6,* "They that sow in tears shall reap in joy." *V-6,* "He that goeth forth and *weepeth,* bearing precious seed, shall doubtless come again with rejoicing, bringing his sheaves with him."

   C. We are told in scripture, that great men of God wept: Esau, Jacob, Saul, David, Peter. The shortest verse in the Bible tells us, "JESUS WEPT." (*John 11:35*) It was at the death of Lazarus. Lack of faith, on the part of his close followers, caused Jesus to weep, here.

"... and a time to laugh;"

1. Here again, people laugh for different reasons. There is the laugh of joy, and the laugh of derision(making fun at someone else's expense). Sarah laughed in derision at the news that she would have a child at 90 yrs.of age. *Gen. 18:13-15.* I honestly believe that she had mixed emotions about this announcement.
2. There will come a time when God will laugh at the folly of the wicked. *Psa. 2:4,Psa. 37:12-13,* and *Prov. 1:25-29.*
3. Laughter means merriment, or a merry heart. *Prov. 15:13* says, "A merry heart maketh a cheerful countenance: but by sorrow of the heart the spirit is broken."
4. *Prov. 17:22,* "A merry heart doeth good like a medicine, but a broken spirit drieth the bones."

"... a time to mourn,"

1. There is a certain amount of comfort in the time of mourning, or deep sorrow and grief. We have an

45

illustration of this in the three friends of Job, who came to mourn with him in *Job 2:11-13*.

2. Here is a very touching scene, of true friends, comforting each other

3. Jesus said, in *Matt. 5:4*, "Blessed are they that mourn: for they shall be comforted."

4. There is coming a time, that mourning will be upon the whole earth, because of the destruction of Babylon. *Rev. 18:11*.

"... and a time to dance;"

1. This is not the Texas Two Step, but dancing for joy, as seen in Psa. 149:1-5 and Psa. 150:1-6. See v-4.

2. In *II Sam. 6:14*, David "danced before the Lord, with all his might." BUT he was not holding someone else's wife, while he was dancing.

3. Evidently he was dancing alone and dancing for joy.

4. There is definitely a sinful side to dancing, for it was by this means that John The Baptist got his head cut off. *Matt. 14:6-8*.

5. Dancing may also glorify God, as seen in *Jer. 31:4,13*. The joy or sorrow of these events depend upon the timing of God. If we do them according to His timing, they bring joy. If not they bring sorrow.

V-5. *"A time to cast away stones,"*

1. The word STONE is found approximately 200 times in the Bible, and used in many different meanings. *Hewn* stone, *living* stone, *precious* stone, *tried* stone, *white* stones, *marble* stones, etc. etc.

2. The heathen hewed themselves images out of stone, and worshiped them, as gods. BUT God forbids this practice in *Lev. 26:1-2*.

3. In *Num. 33:51-53*, God told Moses to destroy all of the pictures, molten images, and high places. The word "pictures", here, probably meant figures chiseled in stone.

4. In *Zech. 7:12* God likens the hard heart to stone.

5. Under the law, stoning was a means of punishing evil doers. *Deut. 13:10, 17:5, 21:21.*

"... *a time to gather stones together;*"

1. Gathering stones was a means of clearing the fields, for agricultural purposes. We find this method used in the parable of the vineyard in *Isa. 5:1-2.*
2. Our good works, after salvation, is called *precious* stones, by the Apostle Paul in *I Cor. 3:12.*
3. They will be gathered together at the Judgement Seat of Christ, along with the wood, hay, and stubble.
4. Another meaning of this phrase could refer to the gathering of *precious* stones, that God will build the walls of the New Jerusalem with in Rev. 21:19.

"... *a time to embrace,*" An expression of commitment, according to Heb. 11:13.

1. This is also an expression of love and friendship. It may also be exercised in time of sorrow. In either case, it is a symbol of sharing our emotions, whether joy or sorrow.
2. In *II Kings 4:16*, Elisha told the Shunammite woman that she would embrace(hold in her arms) a son. This was in reward for her faithfulness.
3. Everybody needs a hug now and then, and this is a meaning (or one of them) of embracing. In Alaska, there are bumper stickers, saying, "Go hug a moose." Now that may be carrying it a bit to far.
4. *Prov. 4:8* tells us, our wives will honor us, if we embrace, or hug them once in a while.
5. The word "embrace" is also applied to receiving a command or doctrine. *Acts 20:1.* Here the words "embraced them" means he exhorted them.

"... *and a time to refrain from embracing;*"

1. You just do not walk up and hug a stranger, and especially strange women. Nowadays she would sue you, for sexual harassment.

47

2. We are warned in *Prov. 5:20* about being ravished by a strange woman, and embracing the bosom of a stranger.

3. *Prov. 2:11* says, "Discretion shall preserve thee, understanding shall keep thee." *V-16* says, "To deliver thee from the strange woman, even from the strange woman that flattereth with her words.

I believe one of the goals we should strive for, in this life, is to find God's timing for everything we do. If we could synchronize our timing with the Lord's, we could walk in harmony with Him. We find the word "time" 28 times in verses 1-8, and every time it is dealing with an event of life.

V-6. "A time to get," This has to do with getting gain, or worldly possessions.

1. There is absolutely nothing wrong with having wealth, if we come by it honestly.

2. We read in *Gen. 13:2*, "And Abram (who was later called Abraham, the friend of God) was very rich in cattle, in silver, and in gold." BUT we also know that Abraham was a man of principle.

3. In *Gen. 14:21-24* we learn something about this man's convictions. He would take nothing from the king of Sodom, lest he say he made Abraham rich.

4. *Prov. 10:22* tells us, "The blessing of the Lord, it maketh rich, and he addeth no sorrow with it."

5. In *I Kings 3:13*, God gave Solomon both riches and honor.

6 *Psa. 112* tells us how we are to treat wealth.

7. We are told to, "Get wisdom, get understanding." *Prov. 4:5-7.*

"... *and a time to lose;*" Or let go of. (turn loose).

1. "...if riches increase set not your heart upon them." *Psa. 62:10b.*

2. "He that trusteth in riches shall fall but the righteous shall flourish as a branch." *Prov. 11:28.*

3. If wealth is lost, due to circumstances over which we have no control, we should not grieve over that loss.
   A. *Prov. 23:5*, "For riches certainly make themselves wings."
   B. *Prov. 27:24*, "For riches are not forever."
4. It is time to loose or let go of wealth, when it takes hold of the owner. *Jer. 9:23*. or, if we forget where it came from. *Deut. 8:17-19*.

"... a time to keep," This is another bible word with several meanings.

l. It means to retain or hold fast. *II Tim. 1:13*. A. Hold fast *sound words. II Tim. 1:13*. B. Hold fast *confidence. Heb. 3:6*. C. Hold fast *our profession. Heb. 4:14 and 10:23*. D. Finally, Jesus said in *Rev. 2:25*, "Hold fast every thing ye have til I come."
2. It means to defend and protect. *Psa. 127:1*.
   A. God said of Jerusalem, "I will defend this city." *Isa. 31:5*, and 37:35.
   B. God will defend the individual. *Psa. 59:1*.
   C. God will defend the poor and fatherless. *Psa. 82:3*.
3. It means to observe and practice. *Psa. 119:4*, and *Acts 16:4*.
4. It means to celebrate. *Matt. 26:18*.

"... and a time to cast away;" Or put away.

1. We have many instances in the Bible, where God has, or will "cast away" certain individuals or nations.
   A. In *John 15:6*; individuals. *Mark 7:26*, the devil.
   B. Israel was cast away for disobedience in *I Kings 9:7*.
   C. God will cast out the heathen. *Psa. 78:55* and *80:8*.
2. God tells us to cast away, or put away some things also.
   A. We are to put away *strange gods. Gen. 35:2*
   B. We are to put away *wickedness. I Cor. 5:13*.
   C. We are to put away *childish things. I Cor. 13:11*.
   D. We are to put away *evil speaking. Eph. 4:31*.

49

V-7.   *"A time to rend,"*

This word has several meanings, but the most applicable, to the christian, is to remove from place, by violence,(to wrest or tear) something from its resting place. As a habit or sin that has taken hold on a christian.

1.   It also has the same meaning as RENT(or tear), as O.T. believers used to do, while grieving. We have an illustration of this in *Gen. 37:29,34.* This is Reuben and Jacob grieving over Joseph.

2.   God used the word "rend" to take the kingdom away from Solomon in *I Kings 11:11.*

3.   When sin gets a strangle hold on a believer, he must "rend" himself, or tear himself away from that sin, as Joel told the People of God to do in *Joel 2:12,13.*

4.   In its truest form, it means "separation". This word is found many times in scripture. Christ was separate from sinners, *Heb. 7:26.* Read *Luke 6:22, II Cor. 6:17.*

"... and a time to sew;" (or mend)

1.   In the case of grieving and mourning, it means to mend the tear made during these times.

2.   A certain amount of grieving is necessary for all believers.

3.   BUT, if cultivated and nourished, it becomes our worst enemy, and a ruinous master.

4.   In *Gen. 4:11-15,* we have the story of Cain, having a pity party and feeling sorry for himself, at the judgement God passed upon him, for killing his brother, Abel.

5.   David said in *Psa. 30:5b,* "Weeping may endure for a night, but joy cometh in the morning."

"... a time to keep silence,"

My mother taught me that a still tongue makes a wise head. You learn more listening than talking.

1.   Remember Jobs friends, in *Job 2:13.* They sat for seven days, without uttering a word. This was one

50

of those times, when silence was golden. They were just there for Job, if he needed them.

2. David knew when to keep silent. *Psa. 39:1-2.*

3. If our opinions expressed, offends others, we must hold our tongue. *James 3:2* is a warning to all. "For in many things we offend all. If any man offend not in *word*, the same is a perfect man, and able also to bridle the whole body."

4. There is a time when we are to put to silence the "foolishness of ignorant men." *I Pet. 2:15.*

5. We learn more when we are silent. Listen to *Job 29:21*, where Job said, "Unto me men gave ear, and waited, and kept silence at my counsel."

BUT THERE IS ALSO "*A TIME T0 SPEAK.*"

1. There is a time to speak out for Christ, or, to witness for Him. *I Thess. 2:4*, "But as we were allowed of God to be put in trust with the gospel, even so *we speak*; not as pleasing men, but God, which trieth our hearts." Read *Acts 1:8, 2:32, 5:32.*

2. In *Acts 4:20*, Peter and John said, "For we cannot but speak the things which we have seen and heard." *V-29.* "And now, Lord, behold their threatenings: and grant unto thy servants, that with all boldness they may SPEAK thy word."

3. In *I Cor.1:10*, concerning the doctrines of Christ, we are told to "all speak the same thing."

4. In *Acts 18:9*, the Lord spoke to Paul at night, in a vision, and said, "Be not afraid, but speak, and hold not thy peace."

5. *Titus 2:1* tells us, "But speak thou the things which become sound doctrine."

This is the seventh lesson on the "*timed* events of life. It will also conclude the study of God pre-determining these events. I believe many of the problems that we have in this life, is brought about because we are out of step with God. They are the result of either getting ahead of God, or following to far behind. Peter got into big trouble with Christ, because he was "following afar off". Matt. 26:58. On the other hand, Enoch walked *with* God(in step and harmony) and got raptured as a reward. *Gen. 5:22-23.* Noah *walked with God* in *Gen. 6:9.* David in *I Kings 9:4.*

V-8.   "*A time to love,*" (Both AGAPE and PHILEO)

1. Love is identified by the deeds or actions it produces.
2. Our word "love" comes from two Greek words: agape and agapao. Agape is a noun, agapao is a verb.
3. Both of these words mean, Divine love, as seen in *John3:16,* and *I John 4:9 10*
4. This is also the kind of love we are to have for the Divine Godhead. Read *John 14:15, 21,23,* and *15:10.*
5. The word Phileo means tender affection, or to be fond of, such as we might have for relatives or close friends. Like "Love thy neighbor as thyself."
6. *Phileo* is never used in a command, to men to love God. It is always *Agape*, that is used, connecting us to God. *Matt. 22:37, Rom. 8:28.*
7. So when we accept Christ as Lord of our lives, it is time to drop the *sentimentality* and *fondness*, and love and serve Him. Far to many "so called" christians, just have a fondness for Christ. BUT GOD KNOWS THE DIFFERENCE.

"*... and a time to hate;*" (like cholesterol, there is the good and bad)

1. The wrong kind of *hate* for the christian, is malicious and unjustifiable feelings toward others, such as is found in *Matt. 10:22, 24:10.*
2. Another wrong kind, for christians, is to hate knowledge. *Prov. 1:29.*
3. The right kind, for a christian, is found in *Psa. 97:10,* "Ye that love the Lord, hate evil."
4. We should hate the things that God hates, and love the things that He loves. God does hate some things. *Prov. 6:16-19, 8:13,17.*

A. *Amos 5:15* tells us to "Hate the evil and love the good."
B. God's word says in *Psa. 119:104,127*, "I hate every false way." Read *Heb.l:9*.

"... *a time of war,*" (a state of hostility) *Luke 14:31*, and *I Kings 14:30*.

1. To the christian, "a time of war" means, a time of spiritual conflict. Paul understood conflict, and instructed Timothy in *-I Tim. 1:18*, to "war a good warfare."
2. *James 4:1* talks about a war (conflict) in the members of the body. Again, war is mentioned in *V-2*. The results are seen in *V-3*.
3. *II Tim. 2:3* encourages us to "endure hardness as a GOOD SOLDIER of Jesus Christ."
4. In *I Tim. 6:12*, "Fight the good fight of faith."
5. When the devil starts pushing us around, it is time to declare war on him.

"... *and a time of peace.*"

1. *Rom. 12:18* tells us, "If it be possible, as much as lieth in you, live peaceably with all men."
2. *Psa. 119:165* says, "Great peace have they which love thy law: and nothing shall offend them."
3. In *Isa. 9:6,7*, our Lord is called the "Prince of Peace."
4. The last part of *Mark 9:50* says, "...have peace one with another."
5. Finally, *Phil. 4:7* tells us, "And the peace of God, which passeth all understanding, shall keep your hearts and minds through Christ Jesus."
6. This comes when we have the PRINCE OF PEACE in our hearts.

V-9. Here in verse nine, Solomon repeats, basically, the same statement he made ill *Ch. 1:13*, meaning, that if we try to plan our lives apart from God, what have we gained at the end of it? Paul said in *I Cor. 15:19*, "If in this life only we have hope in Christ, we are of all men most miserable." It is here in this life that we lay up treasures for heaven." IF on the other hand, we find God's timing for our lives, then we believe that God will also determine the CONDITIONS of life here and hereafter. We know that the condition of life, here and in eternity, depends on our relationship to Jesus Christ.

V-10.   *"I have seen the travail,"* (physical and mental exertion)

In scripture, this word is used in connection with a woman during child birth. Psa. 48:6, Jer. 6:24, and 22:23. Man travails in labour, but for the wrong things. Jesus tells us what to labour for in *John 6:27.*

"... which God hath given to the sons of men to be exercised in it."

This all started in the garden of Eden, back in *Gen. 3:17-19.* Adam fell out of favor with God, in a moment of weakness, and we are all paying for that sin of disobedience. I believe man brings most of his problems, in this life, upon himself; as the beautiful old hymn says, "O what *needless* pains we bear, all because we do carry *everything* to God in prayer."

V-11.   *"He hath made everything beautiful in his time:"*

This phrase refers to the creation, where God said in *Gen. 1:31,* "And God saw everything that he had made, and, behold, it was very good (beautiful). This was BEFORE man sinned and messed it all up.

V-11.   *"... also he hath set the world in their heart,"*

He has given man the intelligence to understand the world of nature, but also to understand the nature of the world. Only a born-again person would understand the nature of the world. The world of nature is God's handiwork, but the nature of the world is the devil's handiwork. *Rom. 1:19-20* includes the world of nature, or the natural things of God's creation. BUT in *II Cor. 4:4,* Satan is called, "The god of this world." Then in *James 1:27,* James said "Pure religion and undefiled before God and the Father is this, to visit the fatherless and widows in their

54

affliction, and to *keep himself unspotted from the world."* Read *I John 2:15-17*. "... *so that no man can find out the work that God maketh from the beginning to the end."*

In other words, man can only understand as much of the world as he is familiar with, and there is a vast amount of the world that he knows nothing about. *Ch. 8:17.* Read *Job 26:14, Rom. 11:33,*

V-12.   *"I know there is no good in them,"*

Remember we are discussing the *works* of man and the *conditions* of life. Apart from God, there is nothing lasting in either. In *Gal. 6:9-10* Paul encourages the people of Galatia, to do the kind of good works that would be lasting and beneficial to themselves, and to those they were helping. THIS KIND OF WORKS IS ALWAYS IN SEASON.

"... but for a man to rejoice, and do good in his life."

This is the purpose of salvation, and the results of God, determining the conditions of this life. Read *2:24.*

V-13.   This verse is a continuation of verse 12, where the preacher said, "I know there is no good in them." He meant, the things that we acquire, the things we labor for. There is no good in them, if we do not enjoy them or thank God for them. The liberty to accumulate things, here on earth and enjoy them, is a gift of God. We are told in *I Cor. 10:13*, "Whether therefore ye eat, or drink, or whatsoever ye do, *do all to the glory of God."* See *Phil. 4:6, I Tim. 4:3-5.*

V-14.   *"I know that whatsoever God doeth it shall be forever:"*

This verse teaches the security of the believer. We believe that God does the saving and the keeping. The words, "for ever" means the same as *eternal* and *everlasting*, and I defy any man to show otherwise. In *Psa. 89:34*, God said, "My covenant will I not break, nor alter the thing that is gone out of my lips."

James 1:17, "Every good gift and every perfect gift(includes salvation) is from above, and cometh down from the Father of lights, with whom is no variableness, neither shadow of turning."

"... *nothing can be put to it, nor anything taken from it:*"

Since man has nothing to do with salvation, he can neither add to or take away from it. *Eph. 2:8-9*, "It is the gift of God, not of works lest any man should boast." God hung the worlds in space, and set the elements in their cycles, and man can do nothing about them. He did all of this that man might fear and respect him, but not all men do.

"... *and God doeth it that men should fear before him.*"

In *Ezek. 36:26-27* God said He would put His Spirit in man. He did not say anything about taking the Spirit out of man. This ought to make man respect God and His power.

Psa. 96:9 reads, "O worship the Lord in the beauty of holiness: FEAR before him, all the earth." The LOST should fear God, and the saved should have a healthy respect for Him.

V-15.   *"That which hath been is now;"*

This phrase simply means that whatever has been in the mind of God in the past, is still there today. We read in *Mal. 3:6*, "For I am the Lord I change not." Perfect memory depends on perfect knowledge, God has both.

"--and that which is to be hath already been;"

This means that whatever God has decreed, it was for all time,past present, and future. Whatever concerns man's future, all the way to infinity. God does not try something for awhile and then change His mind, and try something else. He has a well ordered plan of Government, because it rests upon the shoulders of Jesus Christ, His Son. *Isa. 9:6* and *verse 7* says, "Of the increase of his government and peace there shall be no end." *Psa. 22:28*, "For the kingdom is the Lord's: and he is the governor among the nations."

"... *and God requireth that which is past.*"

In other words, history repeats itself. God has passed judgement upon man in the past, and requires more judgement in the future. God also requires the obedience of the Patriarchs of old to be manifest in every generation. He also promises blessing, to those who exercise obedience. *Isa. 1:19*, "If ye be willing and obedient, ye shall eat the good of the land."

V-16. *"And moreover I saw under the sun the place of judgement,"*

Bear in mind, that the words "under the sun" refers to earthly things and scenes. The place where justice and righteous judgement should be administered. But the sad truth is:

"... that wickedness was there."

The Apostle Paul warns christians as to who their enemies would be in *Eph. 6:12*. Crooked lawyers and judges are not confined to the television set, but are a reality in our courthouses across America. They forget that *Hosea 7:2* is still in the book, which reads, "And they consider not in their hearts that I remember all their wickedness: now their own doings have beset them about: they are before my face." God saw mans wickedness in the old world, in *Gen. 6:5-7*. He corrected it then, and rest assured, He will correct the wickedness of this present world. He knows all about the wickedness of man, for we read in *I John 5:19*, "And we know that we are of God, and the whole world lieth in wickedness."

If iniquity was found only in the world, it would be a different story, but we read:

"... and the place of righteousness, that iniquity was there."

Iniquity (lawlessness) has invaded the so-called churches across our nation and the world. Preachers have "sold out" to the god of mammon, and we now have homosexual congregations that call themselves churches, all over America. God have mercy!! God has their number according to *Isa. 5:20-23* and *Rom. 1:24-28*. JESUS warns against false prophets in *Matt. 7:15* where He said, "Beware of false

57

prophets which come to you in sheep's clothing, but inwardly they are ravening wolves." Also see the scriptures in *Matt. 24:11,24* concerning false prophets.

V-17.   *"I said in mine heart, God shall judge the righteous and the wicked:"*

This does not occur at the same time, but will take place, regardless of the time between them. Regardless of how corrupt our elected officials may be, there is still a higher judge, that they will answer to. Read *Ezek. 7:27* and *Isa. 40:23b* tells us "He maketh the judges of earth as vanity." *Psa. 96:13* says, "He shall judge the world with righteousness, and the people with his truth." *Rev.19:11* tells us, "In righteousness he doth judge and make war."

"... for there is a time there for every purpose and FOR EVERY WORK."

God is a God of purpose. Everything God does, He does with intention, resolution, and determination. This is the meaning of *Prov. 20:18*, "Every purpose is established with counsel: and with good advice make war." Listen to *Jer. 51:29*, "The land shall tremble and sorrow: for every purpose of the Lord shall be performed against Babylon, to make the land of Babylon a desolation without an inhabitant." God judges the intent of the heart, or the reason we do anything. Read *Heb. 4:12*.

V-18.   *"I said in mine heart"*

Here in *verse 18* he starts with the same words that he used in V-17. In V-17 he wants man to know that God will judge all classes, without exception. Here in V-18 we find a second solution to man's problem, if he would accept it. This is:

"... concerning the estate of the sons of men, that God might manifest them,"

God wants man to see his true nature, as a fallen creature. Man, in his fallen state, is as helpless as an animal, to lift himself from that condition. This is the meaning of the words:

"*... that they might see that they themselves are beasts.*"

"Sons of men" always means "sons of Adam" or men still in the old Adamic nature only. He may be intelligent and even righteous, in his own estimation, but *Isa. 64:6* gives God's idea of our goodness. He said, "But we are ALL as an unclean thing (in the old nature) and all our righteousness are as filthy rags; and we all do fade as a leaf; and our iniquities, like the wind, have taken us away." (from God, that is.)

V-19. "*For that which befalleth the sons of men (referring to the old Adamic nature) befalleth beasts.*"

In V-18, God wants man to see that as far as helping himself up from the fall, he is as helpless as a beast or animal. Just as animals are of temporary existence, here on earth, so is man. As a matter of fact, Paul tells us in *Eph. 2:1-3*, that in our fallen nature, we are dead to God. See also *Eccl. 9:12*; *Psa. 49:12,20*; *Psa. 73:22*. Apart from God, man and beast alike, are subject to their nature, which controls them.

"*... even one thing (or the same thing) befalleth them:*"

According to *Heb. 9:27* death is waiting to claim man, and we know the same fate awaits the animal creation, (minus the judgement).

"*... as the one dieth, so dieth the other;*"

Man has no superiority over beasts, when death comes calling.

"*... yea, they have all one breath;*"

That is, the breath of life, that God gave them. *Gen. 6:17, Acts 17:25.*

"*... so that a man hath no preeminence above a beast; for ALL is vanity.*"

Meaning that with all of mans skill, planning, strength, and cunning, he can not escape death. BUT he can prepare for it, here on earth, that in the next life, he will not have the fear of death. See *I Cor. 15:39-50.*

V-20.   *"All go unto one place; all are of the dust, and all turn to dust again."*

In *Gen. 3:19*, God promised Adam that because of his disobedience, he would return to the dust of the ground, from which he had been made. *Gen. 2:7.* Man and beast return to the ground, but the spirit returns to God. *Eccl. 12:7.* In *Num. 16:22* we find these words, "0 God, the God of the spirits of all flesh."

V-21.   *"Who knoweth the spirit of man that goeth upward, and the spirit of the beast that goeth downward to the earth?"*

In searching the scriptures, we find no evidence that God will resurrect the animal kingdom. Here in V-21, it is clear to me that the spirit of man goes upward, while the spirit of animals die and go into the earth, with the body. As far as escaping death, they are the same, but as for their eternal destiny, the spirit of man returns to God. However, there will be animals in the kingdom age. *Isa. 11:6, and 65:25.*

Paul tells us in *II Cor. 5:8*, "We are confident, I say, and willing rather to be absent from the body, and to be present with the Lord." *Phil. 1:21*, "For to me to live is Christ, but to die is gain." How so? To live here is to live FOR Him, but to die in the Lord is to live WITH Him. Paul said in *Phil. 1:23*, "For I am in a strait betwixt two, (conflicting desires) having a desire to depart, and to be with Christ which is far better." *Prov. 15:24*, "The way of life is above to the wise, that he may depart from hell beneath." *Psa. 29:14-15.*

V-22.   *"Wherefore I perceive that there is nothing better, than that a man should rejoice in his own works;"*

I believe God fully intended for man to enjoy the fruits of his labor, here on earth, as he stated in *Eccl. 2:24.* However he can only do this, if he honors God in his acquisition of material things. "This I saw that it was from the hand of God." God is not endorsing sinful Pleasures here, but encouraging us to be thankful for such things as we have. *Col. 3:15*, "Let the peace of God rule in your hearts, to the which also ye are called in one body; and be ye thankful."

"... *for that is his portion (from God, 5:18); for who shall bring him to see what shall be after him,*"

Who among men can make known the future apart from the word of God. ONLY God can make known the future through His Holy Word.

Chapter 4

Verses 1-3 of chapter 4 discusses evil oppression of those outside the family of God. Those who have no comforter.

V-1. *"So I returned,*

From where? In chapter three, verses 16-22, we have discussed the fact of wickedness in the places of judgement; and even in the places where righteousness is supposed to be found, and the fact that God judges all. Here in chapter four verse one, the Preacher returns to that subject, to explore the problems of oppressions from man to man. *"... and considered all the oppressions that are DONE UNDER THE SUN:"* Job had a problem with oppression in *Job 35:9*, but found the answer. To oppress someone means to burden or crush them by abuse of power or authority. Oppression is a sense of being weighed down in body or mind. David writes about this in *Psa. 12:1-8. Eccl. 5:8* tells us, God sees it. Read *Eccl. 7:7.*

"... and behold the tears of such as were oppressed,"

Not only did Solomon take note of the tears of the oppressed, but God also takes note. We are told in *Isa. 38:5* that He saw the tears of old Hezekiah, and extended his life 15 years. *Rev. 7:17* and *21:4* tells us that God will one day wipe away all tears, that there will be no tears after *Rev. 21:4.*

"... and they had no comforter;"

My heart goes out to all the poor and oppressed, in this life, and yet are lost and have only eternity in hell to look forward to. But praise God, the believer is promised the Comforter, which is the Holy Ghost in *John 15:16 and John 16:7-11.*

"... and on the side of the oppressors there was POWER but they had no COMFORTER."

Neither the oppressed nor the oppressors had the comforter. They are in the condition that Jesus speaks of in *Matt. 15:14*, about the blind leading the blind, and both falling in the ditch. The oppressors of this world will get their come-uppance. *Psa. 27:12, 14, 16, 20, 21, 32, 34, 35, and 40.* See *Psa. 101:8* and *75:10*. The oppressors have power, but not from God. *II Thess. 2:3-10.*

V-2.   In view of all the oppression and evil which happens to man(apart from God), he is better off dead, until you look at it from the prospect of judgement. The Preacher said back in chapter two, "Therefore I hated life; because the work that is wrought under the sun is grievous unto me; for all is vanity and vexation of the spirit." We believe Solomon is referring to the saved, here in verse two. They are the only ones who would be better off dead than alive.

V-3.   *"Yea, better is he (dead christian) than both they, (oppressed and* oppressors of V-1) *which hath not yet been (born) who hath not seen the evil work that is done under the sun."*

Verse three becomes a reality only if the central point of our existence is in this life. It also gives meaning to *I Cor. 15:19.* But for the believer, *Rev. 14:13* tells us, "Blessed are the dead which die in the Lord from henceforth. Yea, saith the Spirit, that they may rest from their labours: and their works do follow them."

V-4.   I believe the key word, in this verse, is the word "envied." The preacher looks at labor from two directions. There are those poor misguided souls, who labor, even in travail and sometimes agony, to have more than anyone else, in order that they might have more than their peers or neighbors. They want to be the Jones that everyone else tries to keep up with. This is PRIDE in one of its worst forms. *I John 2:16* calls it the PRIDE OF LIFE, and says it is not of the Father, but of the world.

Then there are those who will not work to better themselves, and yet are envious of those who do work, and are successful. The bible calls this type of person, SLOTHFUL, and gives the results of a slothful (lazy) person in *Prov. 24:30-34*. Envy is brother to that green-eyed monster called jealousy, and no one will ever prosper if they harbor it in their heart.

Listen to *Job:5:2*, "For wrath killeth the foolish man, and envy slayeth the silly one." *Prov. 14:30*, "A sound heart is the life of the flesh: but envy the rottenness of the bones." See what *James 3:14,16* says about envy. The motive for success should never be envy and jealousy, because success itself is no guarantee of happiness.

V-5.   *"The fool foldeth his hands together, and eateth his own flesh."* WHAT DOES THIS MEAN? Simply this, the lazy person brings ruin upon themselves. *Prov. 6:9-11*. In folding his hands together and refusing to work, he would, normally, starve to death. This is what *II Thess. 3:10* says should happen to him.

V-6.   One handful of peace of mind and quietness, is better than both hands full of unrest and anxiety. *Prov. 15:16* puts it another way, "Better is little with the fear of the Lord, than great treasure with trouble therewith." *Prov. 16:8*, "Better is little with righteousness than great revenues without right."

V-7.   *"Then I returned and I saw vanity under the sun."*

Verses seven and eight go together for the VANITY is in laboring for self alone, without anyone to share life with.

V-8.   *"There is one alone,"*

This means, going through life, with no one to be a part of it. This type of person works to gather riches, but the truth is:

"Neither is his eye satisfied with riches;"

Wealth, alone, never brings lasting satisfaction. GREED is the reason for this. *Prov. 27:20* tells us this, "Hell and destruction are never full; so the eyes of man are never satisfied." Show me a miser, and I'll show you a person without friends. *Psa. 39:6* describes this type of person. "Surely every man walketh in a vain show: surely they are disquieted in vain: he heapeth up riches, and knoweth not who shall gather them."

This scripture should serve as a warning to every person trying to get through this world, with no responsibility to anyone. The writer says, *"This also is vanity, yea, it is a sore travail."* It is a useless and worthless existence. On the other hand, *Prov. 11:24* says, "There is (the attitude) that scattereth, and yet increaseth; and there is that (attitude) withholdeth more than is meet, and it tendeth to poverty."

The subject of the "vanity of hard work with the wrong motive," is continued in verses 9-12. The Nelson Bible calls verses 4-12, "The Folly Of Hard Work." But there is nothing foolish about hard work. With the right motive, it is a rewarding experience.

V-9.　　This verse is connected to V-8, and the phrase, *"There is one alone and there is not a second."* Meaning, no one to share our life with makes for a lonely existence. Loneliness is a terrible companion. It bereaves the soul. V-8.

"Two are better than one; because they have a good reward for their labour."

There is an old proverb that says, "Two heads are better than one." There are times when two people, working together, will produce more than twice what one could, by themselves. Then there is the added attraction of companionship, when two or more work together. But there are exceptions to every rule. This verse is also connected to verse 10.

V-10　*"For if they fall, the one will lift up his fellow:"* (if he is strong enough).

We have the beautiful illustration of the war between the Israelites and Amalek in *Exod. 17:8-16,* where Aaron and Hur held up Moses' hands, so Joshua could win the battle.

"... but woe to him that is alone when he falleth;"

66

Simply because there is no one to help him up. There is another reason, seen in *Rom. 14:7*, where we are told, "For none of us liveth to himself, and no man dieth to himself." (If he is a christian).

Christians are to live for the Lord, and each other, if so we never die alone. *Psa. 23:4*, "Yea, though I walk through the valley of the shadow of death, I will fear no evil: for thou art with me; thy rod and thy staff they comfort me." We just step out of this life, and through a door, into the next life. *Phil. 1:21*, "For to me to live is Christ, and to die is gain." Then *II Cor. 5:8* tells us that to be "absent from the body is to be present with the Lord."

V-11. *"Again, if two lie together, then they have heat:"* This speaks of creature comfort, as King David's servants sought for him, in *I Kings 1:1-4*. They had good intentions. It is a fact that, two bodies together, will generate heat, while one, alone, will lose body heat. I have read of dog mushers sleeping, surrounded by their sled dogs, to keep from freezing to death.

"... but how can one be warm alone."

He can't if it's very cold, and he has insufficient covering.

V-12. While V-11 deals with creature comfort, this verse deals with *creature safety*. One big man may attack a smaller man and overcome him, but two small guys probably could overcome the larger man. I am reminded of the little man who was hit by a rotten tomato, and asked, "Who flang that mater?" A big man stepped out from behind a tree, and said, "I did." The little man said, "Man, you sho is a good mater flanger." Or the little umpire who was calling balls and strikes, behind a big catcher, and a big batter. He called two, and the batter and the catcher, both asked, "Two what?" He said, "Too close to call."

Prov.11:14, "Where no counsel is the people fall: but in the multitude of counselors there is safety."

Col. 2:19, "And not holding the head, from which all the body (church) by joints and bands having nourishment ministered, and knit together, increaseth with the increase of God."

In *Matt. 18:19-20* Christ tells us that two or more people constitutes the presence of God. Then in *Luke 10:1* Jesus sent the 70 disciples out in pairs, for the reason we have in the book of Ecclesiastes.

"... and a threefold cord is not quickly broken."

A single thread is easily broken, but when you twist three strands together, they are difficult to break. There is another application to this threefold cord, and that is the threefold security of the believer, by the Father, Son, and Holy Ghost. This is referred to in Matt. 28:19. Also in John 10:27-29 which lists two of the Divine Persons responsible for our security.

In verses 13-16 we learn that power, authority, and popularity are never permanent, and may even be short lived.

V-13.　It is possible that Solomon is referring to himself, when he speaks of the *old and foolish king,* who will no longer listen to good advice, or be admonished (heed a warning). It has been said, "there is no fool like an old fool." We know that God warned Solomon twice, right after he was made king. Once, in *I Kings 3:14* and again in *I Kings 9:2-9.* Before Solomon died he lost his wisdom for disobeying God. One of the truths, taught here, is that young people hunger for knowledge, and are teachable. This is the reason God tells us to teach His word to our children, in *Deut. 6:4-9* and *11:18-19.*

In *Luke 2:42-46* we find Jesus in the temple, learning the scriptures, at the age of 12 years. However, before we can teach others, we must have a teachable spirit; such as Job had, though he was an old man. Read *Job 6:24* and *34:32.* In *Psa. 27:11*, David said, "Teach me thy way, O Lord, lead me in a plain path, because of

68

mine enemies." Many old people, just don't like to exercise their imagination. *Acts 2:17* tells us, they like to "dream dreams."

V-14.   "*For out of prison he* (the poor and wise child) *cometh to reign;*"

We have an illustration of this very thing happening, in the person of Joseph. He was in prison in Egypt, but was released and became ruler and second in command, under Pharaoh. *Gen. 41:14,41-43.* A child may be shackled at birth, with poverty and circumstances beyond their control, but they do not have to remain there all their lives.

Here in our lesson, a poor but wise child trades places with a *king, and finds his way from a prison to a throne.* BUT his popularity soon fades, and his kingdom suffers for it, and those born during his reign, become impoverished. He came from humble beginnings to the pinnacle of success, and was very popular by those who elected him, but soon lost that popularity. Could we not apply this scenario to our current President Bill Clinton?

V-15.   "*I considered all the living which walk under the sun,* (that is, all those who were subject to the youthful king, who succeeded the old one, and fared no better) with the second child that shall *stand up in his stead.*"

This means that the Preacher looks at the complete picture from the old and foolish king, to his youthful successor (second child). Verse 16 gives the results of his findings.

V-16.   It seems to me, that the meaning of V-16 is, that regardless of who is reigning as king or leader, the people soon tire of him, and seek his successor.

The bottom line is, humanity is never satisfied, and this leads to vanity and vexation of the spirit.

The answer to these verses, is found in *Psa. 37:1-6, Gal. 6:9,* and *Matt. 25:21.*

Chapter 5

In the closing verses of chapter four, we discovered a great truth about popularity; that it is often times very temporary, and may even become a snare to those who seek it. As *Prov. 31:30* tells us, "Favour is deceitful, beauty is vain." Yet we are encouraged, from the scriptures to seek favour with God. MOSES sought God's favour in *Num. 11:11*. MARY (the Lord's mother) found favour with God: *Luke 1:30*. DAVID found favour with God; *Acts 7:45-46*. Here in chapter five, we are instructed in the vanity of human religion or outward appearances.

V-1.   *"Keep thy foot when thou goest to the house of God,"*

This means watch your step, or as Paul puts it in *Eph. 5:15*, "See then that ye walk circumspectly, not as fools ..." In other words, remember where you are, that you are in the sanctuary of God, and act accordingly. *Psa. 77:13* says, "Thy way O God, is in the sanctuary: who is so great a God as our God." (The one we meet in His house or sanctuary). In *Psa. 63:1-2*, David longed to see God's glory in the sanctuary. Read *Psa. 119:59, 105; Prov. 1:15; Prov. 4:26-27*.

"... and be more ready to hear than to give the sacrifice of fools:"

One sacrifice the fool makes, is in giving LIP service only, to God, without the heart being involved. We are told in *I Sam. 15:22* that obeying the voice of God, is better than sacrifices. The same thought is taught in *Prov. 21:3, Jer. 7:23*. When we come to the house of God, we should be more ready to listen than to talk, unless we are the teacher or the preacher. Even then, we are to listen to any and all *sincere* questions from the audience. It is good to ask questions, then listen quietly to the answer and weigh the answer according to the scriptures.

"... *for they consider not that they do evil.*" (they, being the fool)

The reason they do not consider their method of worship, to be wrong or evil, is because of what God told Isaiah in *Isa. 44:20*, "He feedeth on ashes: a DECEIVED heart hath turned him aside, that he cannot deliver his soul, nor say, is there not a lie in my right hand?" Jesus said in *Luke21:8*, "Take heed that ye be not deceived." In *II Tim 3:13*, Paul warns Timothy that in the last days, before the Lord's coming, that, "Evil men and seducers shall wax worse and worse, deceiving and being deceived." Read *II Thes. 2:9-12, Rom. 1:26-28.*

V-2.   "*Be not rash with thy mouth,*"

This word "rash" means, undue haste, or lack of deliberation or caution. It means put your BRAIN in gear before you start your mouth to running. In *Acts 19:36* the town clerk of Ephesus told the people, "Seeing then that these things cannot be spoken against, (concerning the things Paul and company was preaching) ye ought to be quiet, and to do nothing rashly." (RECKLESSLY)

"*... and let not thy heart be hasty to utter anything before God:*"

How many times could wrongs be prevented, if we would just stop and think, before we respond to a question or statement? *Prov. 14:29* tells us, "He that is slow to wrath is of great understanding; but he that is hasty of spirit exalteth folly." *Prov. 29:20*, "Seest thou a man that is hasty in his words? There is more hope of a fool than of him."

"*... for God is in heaven and thou upon the earth; therefore let thy words be few.*"

See *Psa. 115:3,16;* and *Isa. 55:8-9; 66:1.*

When we go to God, in prayer, we are to remember that He is on the Throne, and we are on the earth, that God has to listen to every person on earth, who is truly

72

saved. Therefore, He does not want to listen to a lot of chit-chat and vain repetitions. Listen to the Lord's discourse of prayer in *Matt. 6:5-8.*

V-3.   This verse is connected to the last phrase of the second verse, "therefore let thy words be few."

"For a dream cometh through the multitude of business;"

When we lay down to sleep, with a lot of heavy stuff on our minds, we are apt to have all manner of images, fleeting phantoms, and even terrifying things hovering over our sub-conscious mind. Dreams are the means whereby our sub-conscious mind is cleared of stress. This is why it is a good thing to let prayer and praise to God be the last thing on our mind before sleep.

"... and a fool's voice is known by multitude of words."

Mal. 2:17 says, "Ye have wearied the Lord with your words." Then there is *Matt. 6:7* where Jesus said, "But when ye pray, use not vain repetitions, as the heathen do: for they think they shall be heard for their much speaking." The meaning seems to be that if we talk long enough or to much, we are liable to sin. *Prov. 10:19* puts it this way, "In the multitude of words there wanteth not sin; but he that refraineth his lips is wise." See also *Eccl. 10:14.*

When we are assembled in the Sanctuary of God, we should seek the unseen and spiritual, the real and supernatural presence of God. If so, this attitude should humble us in a spirit of *reverence* and *awe*, that the Sovereign God would meet with us. See *Gen. 28:16-19, Psa. 89:7* and *Isa. 6:1-5.*

God's presence among us should bring a hush upon our spirit. *Hab. 2:20* says, "But the Lord is in His holy temple: let all the earth keep silence before him."

Zech. 2:13 tells us to, "Be silent, O all flesh, before the Lord: for he is raised up out of his holy habitation." In *Psa. 85:8* David said, "I will hear what the Lord God will speak: for he will speak peace unto his people, and to his saints: but let them not turn again to folly."

What God desires of His people, is not the outward offering of sacrifices and the celebrating of ceremonies, but the INWARD devotion of our spirit. Read *I Sam. 15:22, Psa. 51:16-17, Jer. 7:21-23,* and *Hos. 6:6.* In *Matt. 23:25-28* the highest form of worship is not speaking of, or giving to God, but HEARING AND RECEIVING FROM GOD.

V-4.   Another example of outward religion and the insufficiencies of it. Yea, even the foolishness of it is making empty promises to God.

"When thou vowest a vow unto God, defer not to pay it;"

Deut. 23:21-23 tells us it is a sin to break our promises to God. After all, you don't have to make God any promises. We are sometimes guilty of making what we call "fox-hole" promises to God. I have made a few of these, myself, when I was in trouble. David understood this in *Psa. 66:13-14.*

I remember that I used to get extremely religious before going into battle, especially during battle, and would make God all kinds of flowery promises, in fact, my mouth wrote a lot of checks, that my body couldn't cash.

Lying to God is a foolish and unprofitable business to be engaged in. Christians cannot afford to get caught in this trap of the devil.

V-5.   Verse five teaches a great practical lesson. When we make promises, concerning God, we had best keep that promise. Nowhere in the bible are we told that we have to make promises to God. *If* you make vows or promises to God, they are voluntary. The KEEPING of those promises is not voluntary. They are mandatory. *Deut. 23:21-23.*

V-6.   *"Suffer not thy mouth to cause thy flesh to sin;"*

What does he mean? I believe he means that the angels are God's witnesses to everything we do or say, because they are always with us. *Psa. 91:11,* "For he (God) shall give his angels charge over thee, to keep thee in ALL thy ways." Verse 12 continues, "They shall bear thee up in

74

their hands, lest thou dash thy foot against a stone."I Cor. 11:10 tells us, "For this cause ought a woman to have power on her head *because of the angels.*" This room is full of angels, because God's people are here, His Word is here, and His Spirit is here. In the Old Testament, the angels even acted as ministers of judgement. EXAMPLE: *Gen. 16:9,13,and 18:2,3.* Also *Exod. 3:2,4.* Notice the second part of that phrase, "*That it was an error.*" In other words, don't do something mean or sinful deliberately, and then try to square it with God. He knew why you done the deed, before you did it. I tried this with my dad, many times, but it never worked. If I accidently hurt one of my sisters, and they went crying to dad, which they always did. I would run ahead of them, and tell dad that I didn't mean to hurt her, but he would not believe me.

He would usually say, "yeah, you little mean dickens, I know you didn't mean to hurt her, just like I don't mean to hurt you with this belt." BELIEVE ME, him saying that did not keep that belt from hurting. "*wherefore should God be angry at thy voice, AND DESTROY THE WORKS OF THY HANDS?*"

Like my earthly father, our heavenly Father punishes us for the attitude, or spirit in which we do our meanness. God's spiritual laws are, many times, carried out by his dealing with our physical lives. *Heb. 12: 5,6; 10,11.*

V-7. Here in verse 7, Solomon sums up the preceding 6 verses, that in mans religion, there is much to-do about dreams and vows; which for the most part, is nothing but superstition. If we try to read something significant into every dream, we end up "nutty as a fruit-cake." Likewise people who are always talking (many words) and making rash promises, makes God weary. *Mal. 2:17,* "Ye have wearied the Lord with your words. Yet ye say, Wherein have we wearied him? When ye say, Everyone that doeth evil is good in the sight of the Lord, and he delighteth in them; or, Where is the God of judgment?" V-7 refers us back to V-2. There is nothing wrong with making vows, or in much speaking, if it glorifies God. IF it does not, it is vanity. *Eccl. 12:13-14* sums up V-7. The very nature of prayer is not in long-winded, flowery words, that flatter God, but in the simplest terms, making known our needs, of body and soul. *Psa. 55:22*, "Cast thy burden upon the Lord, and he shall sustain thee: he shall never suffer the righteous to be moved." *Phil. 4:6*, "Be careful (anxious) for nothing; but in everything by prayer and supplication with thanksgiving let your requests be known unto God."

Here in verses 8-12, we learn another very important lesson about this life, "under the sun" or here on earth. We learn that wealth and worldly possessions do not satisfy. The first part of verse 8 is referring back to *Chapter 3:16*, where Solomon found "wickedness" and "iniquity" in the places of judgement and righteousness. Meaning, our courts and so-called churches.

V-8.   *"If thou seest the oppression of the poor,"*

This word means, unjust or cruel exercise of authority or power. One example of this, is turning criminals out early and putting them back on the streets, to prey on the innocent children and adults. I am in agreement with *Eccl. 7:7* which says, "Surely oppression maketh a wise man mad." Not only should it make him angry, but enough oppression will drive a wise man crazy, which is the true term used here, for mad. In *Psa. 119:134* David prayed, "Deliver me from the oppression of man: so will I keep thy precepts."

It is sad but true, that there is such a thing as RELIGIOUS OPPRESSION. Jesus warns about this kind of oppression in *Matt. 23:4* and *Luke 11:46*. I believe that Roman Catholicism is the leading culprit in the practice of religious oppression of its poor members. The poorest countries in the world, are predominantly Catholic. While its members are wallowing in poverty, the Vatican City is sitting on BIL-LIONS of dollars in gold bullion.

"*... and violent perverting of judgement and justice in a province, marvel not at the matter:*"

Solomon tells us not to be surprised or dismayed, if we find these things in places of higher authority, because it is just the fulfillment of Eph. 6:10-11.

However, the POOR have this consolation: "*... he that is higher than the highest regardeth; and there be higher than they.*"

Take notice of, and pay attention to Psa. 102:17. Thanks be to God, He knows all about these things, and will one day set the record straight. Read *I Sam. 2:7-10, Job 5:15-16, Job 36:15, Psa. 9:18, and Psa. 12:5-8.* God is still on the throne, and still in charge, and soon all accounts will be settled.

V-9.   "*Moreover the profit of the earth is for all:*"

If all men believed and practiced this, the wealth of the world, and the good life would be shared by all. I am convinced, that this is the reason God put all the minerals and resources in and on the earth, that everyone could enjoy them. After all, He is the owner of all the wealth of the universe, but He tells us in *Mal. 3:8-9* that man has ROBBED Him of this wealth, and has taken it and squandered it upon himself. Moses reminds us in *Deut. 8:17-19* who owns what. *I Cor. 10:24* says, "Let no man seek his own, but every man anothers wealth." HOW MANY PRACTICE THIS?

By the way, this does not mean, seek every man's wealth, to try to get it from him, but to add to his wealth.

I wish, you men of the church, would pay attention to this verse, and start adding to the preacher's wealth. In all seriousness, *Psa. 50:10-12* tells us that God is the owner of the cattle on a thousand hills.

"*... the king himself is served by the field.*"

From the king to the peasant, all are to partake of what the earth provides for man.

When Solomon said in the last part of verse 9, "The king himself is served by the field", he is telling us, that there are some things better than money in the bank (for one thing, you can't eat it). The soil produces products for every area of life. Even the king depends on the industry of his subjects. Therefore, if he oppresses his people, he hurts his own revenues. *Prov. 12:11*, "He that tilleth his land shall be satisfied with bread: but he that followeth vain persons is void of understanding.

V-10.   *"He that loveth silver shall not be satisfied with silver;"*

It is a known fact that the more wealth a person has, the more they want, and the more they worry about keeping what they already have. Wealth has a way of deceiving its owners, many times. Read *Psa. 49:6-7; 16-17; I Tim. 6:10*. The "love of money" is fostered by that green-eyed monster called "greed." *Psa. 37:16* tells us that, "A little that a righteous man hath is better than the riches of many wicked." *Psa. 39:6* shows the folly of seeking riches as the main goal in life. See also *Psa. 52:7; Psa. 62:10*.

On the other hand, God honors those who fear Him, and honor HIM with their wealth. *Psa. 112:1-3*.

"... nor he that loveth abundance with increase: this also is vanity." (empty and vain)

The meaning seems to be, that the man that already has an abundance of wealth, and keeps wanting to increase them, is vain and empty, and guilty of covetousness. *Prov. 27:20* hits the nail on the head, when it says, "Hell and destruction are never full; so the eyes of man are never satisfied."

In *I Chron. 29:16-17* David realized that everything they (God's people) possessed belonged to God, and offered it back to God.

V-11.   *"When goods increase (in times of plenty), THEY ARE INCREASED that eat them:"*

When fields produce abundantly, it takes more hands to harvest the crops, and of course, more mouths to feed.

"... and what good is there to the owners thereof saving the beholding of them with their eyes."

If sitting back and looking at one's wealth is the main objective in having it, then there is no advantage in acquiring it. If on the other hand we accumulate wealth to help the needy, and to share with those less fortunate than we, then God will reward that spirit. *Psa. 13:7* tells us, "There is that maketh himself rich, YET hath nothing: there is that maketh himself poor, yet hath great riches." WHAT IS THE DIFFERENCE? The ATTITUDE with which we approach wealth. *Prov. 13:11*, "Wealth gotten by vanity shall be diminished: but he that gathereth by labour shall increase."

V-12. *"The sleep of the labouring man is sweet,"* After a hard days work, whether physical or mental, there is nothing better than a good nights rest, to refresh and restore the body to health.

On the contrary, the sleep of the sluggard, brings poverty. *Prov. 6:9-11.*

"... but the abundance of the rich will not suffer him to sleep."

Because he is to concerned about keeping his wealth, or how to make more. For a person like this, it is hard to relax their mind, that they might enjoy a good nights rest. They sleep as it were, with one eye open.

In previous verses we have discovered that wealth does not satisfy, and may be harmful to its owner. Many who attain great wealth, indulge in the fleshly pleasures of this life, to the destruction of their health, and die premature deaths.

V-13. The words "*sore evil*", here means *very bitter*, or painful difficulties. Wealth, stored up for the owners use only, does not satisfy him. Even more evil, is the fact that it helps no one else. I read in the paper, not long ago, about the elderly "bag lady" who lived on the streets of N.Y. City, begging all of her life, and died with over two

79

hundred thousand dollars ($200,000) in her meager possessions. Of course, the city got her savings. We are reminded of *Psa. 37:16; and 39:6.*

David, the man after God's own heart (*Acts 13:22*), gives a good example of how to use wealth in I *Chron. 29:10-13,28.*

V-14.   *"But those riches perish by evil travail:"*

This word "travail" means "physical or mental exertion." Meaning, that some poor souls really work at being stingy. The real meaning here is that riches may vanish, by any number of ways; such as storms, fires, floods, even robbers and law suits. If the truth be known, probably more people loose their wealth by lawyers than bandits. The fact remains that some people cannot handle the sudden loss of wealth. The stock market crash of 1929 is a prime example, when many committed suicide

"... and he begetteth a son, and there is nothing in his hand."

If the one who looses his wealth has children, he leaves nothing for an inheritance.

V-15.   This verse verifies the fact, that "you can't take it with you." There is a scriptural foundation for that saying. *Psa. 49:16-17*, "Be not thou afraid when one is made rich (that he will take it to the grave with him), when the glory of his house is increased." V-17, "For when he dieth he shall carry nothing away: his glory shall not descend after him." Here in V-15, Solomon concurs with *Job 1:21*, where Job said, "Naked came I out of my mother's womb, and naked shall I return."

The Apostle Paul reaffirms this in *I Tim. 6:7*, when he told Timothy, "For we brought nothing into this world, and it is certain we can carry nothing out." Then verse 8 of this same book tells us, "And having food and raiment let us be therewith content."

V-16.　Here V-15 is repeated that, "*in all points as he came, so shall he go.*" NAKED AND HELPLESS.

"*... and what profit hath he that hath laboured for the wind?*"

Absolutely none! The writer is just repeating the conclusion he reached, back in *Eccl. 2:11,22 and 3:9.* Jesus gives an illustration to the meaning of these verses, in the parable of the RICH FOOL, in Luke 12:13-21.

V-17.　"All his days also he eateth in darkness,That is, in ignorance of what his wealth could have accomplished, had he used it wisely.

"*... and he hath much sorrow and wrath with his sickness.*"

"Sickness" here is covetousness and greed, that is like a cancer, eating away at the soul of man. As Paul said in *I Tim. 6:9*, "But they that will be rich fall into temptation and a snare, and into many foolish and hurtful lusts, which drown men in destruction and perdition."

In verses 18-20, we learn some of the greatest truths, found in the Bible, concerning wealth and satisfaction with life here on earth. Paul gives us the key to being satisfied with life, in *Phil. 4:11-13* and *I Tim. 6:8* where he said, "And having food and raiment let us be therewith content."

V-18.　"*Behold that which I have seen:*"

I believe when Solomon penned these words, he was speaking from experience, for he had tried everything that wealth could bring. Read *Eccl. 2:3.* Here we are told that he tried enjoyment through worldly pursuits, and found vanity (emptiness). In V-3, he tried wine, wisdom, and folly (foolishness). Verse 18 refers to the labouring man. The preacher re-affirms what he learned back in chapter 2:24, that everything we have, in this life, comes from the hand of God. Whether we have little or much, we are to be satisfied with it and give God the glory for it. I believe *I Tim. 6:6* is the key to happiness. Paul told Timothy that, "Godliness with contentment is great gain." Then in *Heb. 13:5* the scriptures tell us, "Let your conversation be without covetousness; and be content with such things as ye have: for he hath said, I will never leave thee, nor forsake thee." No man can enjoy the good of all that he labors for, in this life, if he is dissatisfied with everything around him and constantly blames others for his unhappiness. The secret is, living every day for the glory of God.

V-19.   This verse refers to the man of wealth, who comes by it honestly and not through oppression of others. One who realizes that his good fortune comes from God. To this type of individual, God also gives the privilege of enjoying his substance.

"... *and to take his portion,*"

I believe this phrase simply means that the man who gives God all the credit for his wealth, takes only his portion, and returns to God, God's portion. This man is the opposite of the Rich Fool in *Luke 12:13-20*. When we compare the Rich Fool in Luke with the man in V-19, of our text, we understand that the fool had "I" trouble. He only loved three people, Me, Myself, and I.

"... *this is the gift of God.*"

It is a gift from God, that man is master of his wealth, and not a slave to it. Some certainly are.

V-20.   "*For he shall not much remember the days of his life;*"

The person who honors God with all that he has, will never look back at the past with remorse and wish he had spent more on himself. On the other hand, he might wish he had given more to God, because of scriptures like *Luke 6:38*, where Jesus said, "GIVE, and it shall be given unto you; good measure, pressed down, and shaken together, and running over, shall men give into your bosom. For with the SAME measure ye mete withal it shall be measured to you again." In *Eccl.*

82

2:11,17 we have the illustration of a man who lived for this life only. The result of his selfish existence is seen in V-17. This man is disappointed and disillusioned with life.

"*... because God answereth him in the joy of his heart.*"

The man who lives for God, in this life, will not look back at the past with regret, and will also not be anxious about the future. He will look forward to eternity, with confidence, trusting in Christ, who told Paul to write in *I Cor. 2:9*, "Eye hath not seen, nor ear heard, neither have entered into the heart of man the things which God hath prepared for them that love him."

God answers our prayers, gives us peace of mind, and a joyous hope for the future. Furthermore, we are encouraged, from the Scriptures, to live life to the fullest, today. *Matt. 6:34* and *James 4:13-14.*

Chapter 6

I believe we could rightly say, that the first two verses of chapter six belong to the previous chapter, because it is the continuation of the subject of wealth. Solomon, who was one of the WEALTHIEST men who ever lived, had learned, from experience, that it was not wealth that brought joy, but the way he used it.

V-1.   *"There is an evil which I have seen under the sun, and it is common among men:"*

This evil which is common among men (everyone is subject to it) is the green-eyed monster, called GREED or COVETOUSNESS. In *I Tim. 6:9-10*, the Apostle Paul warns Timothy about falling into this trap (snare). Notice also in V-9 the phrase, "They that will be rich." This is the person that has their mind set on wealth, and are usually not to particular how they get it. There is no evil in money, perse; but the evil is in the LOVE of money. Paul said it is the ROOT of all evil. It is the COVETING after money, that pierces men through with many sorrows. We are told in *Psa. 62:10b*, "If riches increase, set not your heart upon them."

There is a great truth taught in *Prov. 13:7* which says, "There is that maketh himself rich, yet hath nothing: there is that maketh himself poor, yet hath GREAT riches." This is what Paul meant in *II Cor. 8:9*, "For ye know the grace of our Lord Jesus Christ, that though he was rich, yet for your sakes he became poor, that ye through his poverty might be made rich."

Prov. 22:1. 4, "A good name is rather to be chosen than great riches, and loving favour rather than silver and gold." V-2 says, "The rich and poor meet together: the Lord is the maker of them all."

YET the lying prophets will tell you, that God does not want anyone to be poor. V-4, "By humility and the fear of the Lord are riches, and honor, and life.."

V-2.   Verse two is the opposite of chapter 5:19. There, God gives the riches, and the power to use them properly, along with the freedom to rejoice in his wealth. However, in V-2, the same God gives wealth, riches, and honor, but does not give him the privilege to enjoy it. WHY?? The difference is in his relationship to God, and his attitude toward his possessions.

In the parable of the rich fool in *Luke 12:16-21.* Jesus called the man a fool in V-20, and tells us in V-21, "So he (a fool) that layeth up treasure for himself, and is not rich toward God."

In *Rev. 18:17* we are warned about the uncertainty of riches. John said, "In one hour great riches can come to naught." (amount to nothing). In the parable of the sower, in Matt. 13, Jesus speaks of the deceitfulness of riches choking the word of God, and keeping us from being fruitful.

"... but a stranger eateth it:"

David sheds light on this in *Psa. 49:6-10.* Then *Job 21:13* says, "They spend their days in wealth and in a moment go down to the grave." *"this is vanity."*

It is emptiness, but even worse than emptiness, it is, *An evil disease.* Like cancer, it can be fatal to a christian.

In V-2, we see a man who has acquired great wealth, but had no heir (a stranger eateth it) and therefore had no lasting benefit in his wealth. Put another way, there is no satisfaction in riches, apart from God, who alone allows us to have them. Now in the next few verses, we are going to learn, that there is no satisfaction in children, apart from God.

V-3.   *"If a man beget an hundred children and live many years,"*

In the days of the O.T., to have a large family, was considered a blessing from God. (I think the figure 100 is just a round number used to express a point). However, there were some quite large families in the Old Testament.

    A. We are told in *II Kings 10:1* that Ahab had 70 sons in Samaria. Probably a few daughters, also.

    B. In *II Chron. 11:21* we find a man, by the name of Rehoboam had 28 sons and 60 daughters. That's a total of 88 children. *How would you like to bring home the bacon to that crew???*

Psa. 127:3 tells us, "Lo, children are an heritage of the Lord: and and the fruit of the womb is his reward." But whether we have 1 or 100, we are told to teach them about God. *Prov. 22:6* says, "Train up a child in the way he should go: and when he is old, he will not depart from it." (his childhood training)

"... and his soul be not filled with good,"

Here is a man that has been blessed with long life and many children, BUT he has lived for the flesh only, and has done nothing for his soul. We are told in *Deut. 11:13,18,19* that we are to serve God with *all our heart and with all our soul.*

That is because the spirit and soul of man is the only part that is eternal, and the part that God works with. *Rom. 8:16*, "The Spirit itself beareth witness with *our* spirit that we are the children of God." *I Thess. 5:23* tells us we are a trichotomous being, made up of spirit, soul, and body.

"and also that he have no burial;"

In the O.T., it was considered a shame and disgrace, to die without a proper funeral service. It was an honor to be buried in the ancestral burial plots of the forefathers. People had a fear of dying and being left on top of the ground, like an animal. We have an illustration of this in *Jer. 22:18-19*. Here, God told the people not to give Jehoiakim a burial ceremony, but to just throw his body outside the gates of Jerusalem.

"I say, that an untimely birth is better than he."

    The preacher tells us that an aborted, or stillborn child is preferred over one whose life and death is so miserable. *Eccl. 4:2-3* sheds more light on this thought of the untimely birth.

V-4.   *"For he cometh in* (to existence) *with vanity and departeth in darkness,"*

    The person who comes into this world, and lives their life selfishly, who never serves God in any way, has wasted two lives. One HERE and the one HERE-AFTER. You see, that person is judged at the Great White Throne, and cast into the lake of fire and brimstone. According to *Eccl. 8:10*, this type of person's life is a life of nothingness, empty and vain. He dies without his life ever having been recorded in the Lamb's book of life. *Rev. 13:8.*

Solomon is comparing the person who has great wealth, many children, and opportunity to use all for lasting good. Yet, if he does not glorify God in ALL that he has, he is no better than a child that is stillborn. In God's sight he is in worse condition because he had an opportunity and failed.

V-5.   The preacher is still referring to the stillborn, that went from the womb to the grave. The advantage that the stillborn has over the stingy miser is, the miserly person affects others. The covetous rich man had an opportunity to do great things for himself and others, and lay up treasures in heaven, that Jesus speaks of in *Matt. 6:19-20.* On the other hand, the baby that went from the darkness of the womb, to the darkness of the grave, has harmed no one, and *"hath more rest* (comfort) *than the other."*

    One has rest from suffering, and the other has NO REST. PERIOD! Read Isa. 57:20-21.

V-6.   *"... yet hath he seen no good:"*

    If a man live twice as long as Methuselah, What has he accomplished? LONGEVITY without CHARITY, is still a wasted life, regardless of how many years he lives. In *I Cor. 13:1-3*, Paul tells us we can do a lot of good things, without CHARITY. However God does not recognize them. In fact, an extended life just adds to the misery. BUT his life here on earth is not the worst part, for:

"... *do not all go to one place?*"

Our station in life, without God, makes absolutely no difference in eternity. *Rev. 6:15-17; Rev. 20:12.*

The lesson here is, that the miserly rich man's wealth has done him no good, here on earth; and even worse, it will not keep him out of hell. We have our lord's warning in *Matt. 19:24.* In *I Tim. 6:7* Paul said, "For we brought nothing into this world, and it is certain we can carry nothing out."

V-7.   In the sixth chapter, according to *Nelsons Bible* (for the most part, I agree with his subject headings) there is no satisfaction in wealth, children, labour, and the future. We understand him to mean apart from God, or when life is lived under the sun, only.

"*All the labour of man is for his mouth,*"

In other words, his foremost need is food for the stomach. But he is not satisfied with food and shelter. This is contrary to Paul's admonishment to Timothy in I Tim. 6:8 where he said, "And having food and raiment, let us be therewith content."

"... *and yet the appetite is not filled.*"

As strange as it may seem, we are told by the Greek scholars, that this word "appetite" comes from the word meaning SOUL, and is the seat of insatiable desires, such as love and hate. The soul is the seat of all of our emotions and desires. Because of these insatiable desires, we learn that man's happiness is not in his own power. We have a great truth taught in *Psa. 128:1-2*, "Blessed is everyone that feareth the Lord; that walketh in his ways." V-2, "For thou shalt eat the labour of thine hands: happy shalt thou be, and it shall be well with thee." See *Eccl. 1:8*. There is an interesting verse of scripture in *Isa. 29:8*, that connects the soul with the appetite.

V-8.   *"For what hath the wise man more than the fool?"*

As for emotions, appetites, and desires, all men are created equal, but the wise man learns to control his emotions. But, is there any advantage in being poor? Not as far as emotions and desires are concerned. The difference, if there is any, seems to be, that the poor man is more apt to rely on God, and trust Him for his livelihood, while the prosperous person is more apt to trust their wealth. As far as what they strive for and desire, they are the same, because money, or lack thereof, does not change man's basic instinct.

So far, in this chapter, we have discussed the lack of satisfaction in wealth (vs.1-2); in children (vs. 3-6); in labour (vs. 7-8). Concerning the subject of labour, *Prov. 16:26* tells us, "He that laboureth laboureth for himself; for his mouth craveth it of him." As far as man is concerned, the primary purpose in working, is not to glorify God, but to sustain self. Now we learn, there is no satisfaction in the future, apart from God.

V-9.   *"Better is sight of the eyes than the wandering of the desire:"*

There is an old saying that says, "A bird in hand is worth two in the bush." There are those who spend their entire lives dreaming of a life of ease and pleasure, and are never satisfied with their station in life. It seems to me that the meaning here is, that it is better to concentrate on the things in sight, than to sit around dreaming about things that may, or may not happen. I believe this is the meaning of *Phil. 4:11* where Paul said, "Not that I speak in respect of want: for I have learned, in whatsoever state I am, therewith to be content." SEE *Heb. 13:5-6*.

"... this is also vanity and vexation of spirit."

The idea of never being contented, in this life, makes life, at the end, empty and vain. On the other hand, living for God and serving Christ, will fill TIME and ETERNITY with joyful surprises. *I Cor. 2:9.*

V-10   *"That which hath been is named already, and it is known that it is man:"*

This idea was discussed in *Eccl. 1:9*, where it is said, "There is no new thing under the sun." Whatever we may encounter, in this life, has been experienced by someone in the past, and there is a name for it. *Acts 15:18* says, "Known unto God are all his works from the beginning of the world."

Since God made man, He knows what man is, and what he is capable of doing or not doing.

"Neither may he (man) *contend with him* (God) *that is MIGHTIER THAN* HE."

Rom. 9:20 and *Isa. 45:9* puts man in his place, before God. At man's best, he is still the CLAY, but God is still the POTTER.

V-11.   *"Seeing there be many things that increase vanity, what is man the better?"*

Though man is the greatest of all of God's creation, and in spite of all man's intelligence, ingenuity, and accomplishments, there is still a cloud hanging over him, because basically, he is VAIN. Man seldom gives God the glory for his accomplishments. Does all of man's existence, here on earth, make him any better prepared for eternity? Not in God's estimation. *II Pet. 2:20* tells us that we only escape the pollutions of the world, through the knowledge of the Lord and Saviour Jesus Christ.

MAN HAS A POLLUTION PROBLEM ALRIGHT, BUT IT IS NOT MUDDY RIVERS AND SMOKEY CITIES. According to *Isa. 1:4-6* and *Isa. 6:5* it is a spiritual problem.

V-12.   *"For who knoweth what is good for a man in this life?"*

Is man capable of planning his own destiny? NO! *Prov. 14:12* tells us, "There is a way which seemeth right unto a man, but the end thereof are the ways of death." To be able to know what is good for him, in this life, he would need to see into the future. We do not know what the future holds, we christians just know who holds the future.

Our life is compared to a "*shadow*" here, and in *James 4:14*, it is compared to a vapor. Whatever the length of this life, if we do not live it for God, it is empty and vain.

"*... for who can tell man what shall be after him under the sun?*" OR, who has gone beyond the vail of death, and returned to tell us what is on the other side??

To have any idea, of what awaits us on the other side of death, we must rely, solely, on God's Eternal Word, such as *I Cor. 15:51-58*.

Chapter 7

In the last part of V-12 of chapter 6, the question is asked, "For who can tell a man what shall be after him under the sun?" There are some things that man will never be able to understand, in this life. "Under the sun." *Job 11;7* poses an interesting question; "Canst thou by searching find out God? Canst thou find out the Almighty unto perfection?" (The depth of His perfection). In *Psa. 139:6* David acknowledged that, "Such knowledge is too wonderful for me; it is high, I cannot attain unto it." FOR INSTANCE: The Deity of God; or the mystery of the Incarnation, etc. In chapter 7 Solomon will compare wisdom (the essential nature of God) with folly.

V-1.   *"A good name is better than precious ointment;"*

Precious ointment would have healing power as well as perfume. *Song of Solomon 1:3.* If we had TO MAKE A CHOICE, which would we choose? *Isa. 1:5* tells us that man is sick in the head and heart. Usually, man would rather *smell good* than *be good.*

Here is another test in *Prov. 22:1*, "A good name is rather to be chosen than great riches, and loving favour (with God) rather than silver and gold." For some people, this would be a hard choice to make, between great wealth or a good name. The writer means? a good name from God's point of view, and not the kind of name that the builders of the tower of Babel wanted to make for themselves in *Gen. 11:4*, In *Acts 11:24* Barnabas was called a *good man.* He no-doubt had a *good name.* In *Luke 23:50* Joseph was a *good man.* He too would have a *good name.*

"... and the day of death than the day of one's birth."

It stands to reason that if we have lived a good life, under the sun, from God's view, we are better off than a new-born who is just beginning life. A good name will continue to inspire others, after we are gone from this life. IN FACT a *good name* may be the ONLY legacy we leave for our children, but we can ALL do that.

At birth, there is the possibility of doing good; at death there is the evidence of a good name, or lack thereof.

REPUTATION and a good name, comes from *character*, which is not what we think of ourselves, nor even what others think of us. It is what we are inside and the sum total of all our choices, made in this life. It has been said, "ONLY ONE LIFE, TWILL SOON BE PAST, ONLY WHAT'S DONE FOR CHRIST WILL LAST."

V-2. *"It is better to go to the house of mourning, than to go to the house of feasting:"*

In the place of feasting or festivities, there is much laughter, but it may be the laughter of fools, mentioned in *V-6*. It may even be in mockery of God. This would be laughter that appeals only to the sensual nature of man, the fleshly nature only. *BUT*, is there a contradiction between this verse and *Eccl. 2:24?* NO! One is the JOY OF SALVATION, the other is the pleasure of sin. On the POSITIVE side of joy and laughter, for the child of God, we turn to *Prov. 17:22*. Another reason that it is better to go to the house of mourning is, there is more serious thinking, contemplation, and meditation. Sorrow and mourning have a place in our lives, but only for a season. See *Psa. 30:11* and *Isa. 22:12*. BUT thank God for *Isa. 51:11,* and *Jer. 31:13*.

"... for that is the end of all men;"

The preacher simply means that all mankind, as far as the flesh is concerned, would rather be in the place of feasting, than the place of sorrow. HOWEVER it also means, that one day, ALL will be mourned, for that is the end result of "life under the sun."

"... and the living will lay it to his heart."

He will take life more seriously when he realizes these truths. See *Eccl. 9:1*. We who are living, should be

94

able to draw profitable conclusions about the brevity of life, and how to make the best use of it.

Our Lord gave us the beatitudes in *Matt. 5*. Verse 4 of that chapter says, "Blessed are they that mourn for they shall be comforted." BUT He also WARNS us in *Luke 6:25b*, when he said, "Woe unto you that laugh now! for ye shall mourn and weep."

Solomon is still contrasting wisdom and folly for the next several verses.

V-3. *"Sorrow is better than laughter:"*

The word "laughter" has a two-fold meaning in the word of God:

1. The laughter of mockery or scorn for the holy things of God, as seen in *Matt. 9:24*. But after V-26, who is laughing now? This same scene is also found in *Mark 5:35-43* and *Luke 8:49-56*. In *Neh. 2:19* the enemies of Nehemiah laughed him to scorn, and even despised him. The world still holds God's people in contempt today. But Jesus said in *John 15:18*, "If the world hate you, ye know that it hated me before it hated you."

2. There is the laughter of joy of God's people. In *Psa. 126:1-2* we find God's people laughing for the joy of being set free. According to V-3, it was the laughter of gladness. Yet even in the midst of joy, we know that sorrow is always near. Listen to *Prov. 14:13* where Solomon said, "Even in laughter the heart is sorrowful; and the end of that mirth is heaviness."

Sorrow is better than laughter for another reason; it causes us to think seriously about the important things of life.

ILLUSTRATION: In *Gen. 3:16-17* God told Eve he would "greatly multiply" her sorrow in child-bearing. I am sure she remembered her disobedience every time she gave birth.

There is such a thing as Godly sorrow. In *II Cor. 7:10* it is compared to the sorrow of the world, "For Godly sorrow worketh repentance to salvation not to be repented of; but the sorrow of the world worketh death."

Then in *I Thess. 4:13* Paul said there was a sorrow which had no hope. Here again, this is the sorrow of the world.

"... for by the sadness of the countenance the heart is made better."

Our countenance is the facial expression of the mood we are in. If there is deep turmoil of the soul, our face will show it. If there is joy in our heart, the face will show that. A sad and dejected look means that person is hurting, and needs comforting, by other christians. Most of all by the COMFORTER HIMSELF, the Holy Ghost, who Jesus promised in *John 16:7-11*. The sympathy of friends and loved ones gives strength, in times of need.

V-4.   *"The heart of the wise is in the house of mourning;"*

The heart of the wise is the person who takes life seriously and is in a position to help others. On the other hand, a person who is always the life of the party and a "hale fellow-well met," is seldom ever prepared to handle tragedy. When he is confronted with the tragedies of life, he falls apart.

In the house of mourning, we face the *brevity of life* and *certainty of death*, and the responsibility of doing the right thing before God.

"... but the heart of fools is in the house of mirth."

The heart of the fool is the person who only thinks of personal gratification, and lives for the present only. The one who seeks to keep life pleasant at all times. This person lives in a fools paradise, and is hard-put to face reality, and the fact that life is not a bed of roses, without the thorns. We are not to go around looking for them, but we should never try to escape the unpleasantries of life.

96

V-5.   *"It is better to hear the REBUKE of the wise than for a man to hear the song of fools."*

Solomon is still on the subject of comparing wisdom and folly. This word "rebuke" means to criticize sharply or reprimand. It is a good bible word, and God uses this means to bring his people back into fellowship, in both the Old and New Testaments.

There is a right way and a wrong way of doing this. We are all familiar with constructive and destructive criticism. One destroys harmony, and even relationships, the other is a manner of critiquing something in order to evaluate it. Destructive criticism just finds fault and denounces everything. In *Luke 17:3*, we are told to rebuke a brother, if he is overtaken in a fault, but to do it in a spirit of forgiveness. Our Lord, Himself, said in *Rev. 3:19*, "As many as I love, I REBUKE AND CHASTEN: be zealous therefore and repent."

In *II Tim. 4:2* Paul exhorts Timothy to, "Preach the word; be instant in season, out of season; reprove, REBUKE, exhort with all longsuffering (patience) and doctrine."

Concerning wisdom, *Prov. 13:1* tells us, "A wise son heareth his father's instruction: but a scorner heareth not rebuke."

FINALLY, listen to *Prov. 17:10*, "A reproof entereth more into a wise man than a hundred stripes into a fool." This verse goes along with the second part of V-5, which says, *"than for a man to hear the song of fools."* I believe all so-called rock music and most contemporary music comes under this category of "song of fools."

Prov. 14:9, "Fools make a mock of sin." Most songs of our day, have absolutely no concept of sin in them. In fact, they encourage and condone sin in the listener. *Prov. 10:23* hits the nail on the head when it says, "It is as SPORT to a fool to do mischief ..." They think it is "cute" or in the common-vanacular, COOL, to toss beer cans and bottles on the church and parsonage lawns. This is a childish way of showing their rebellion, against God and His church. There are the songs of the devil's crowd, that are full of profanity and sacrilege, toward God. THANK GOD there are beautiful sacred hymns of praise to our Lord, that inspire the hearers.

V-6.   *"For as the crackling of thorns under the pot;"*

This statement refers back to the custom, in the old days, of burning grass, stubble, and thorns for heat. Thorns, as heating material, is mentioned in *Psa. 58:9*, and *Psa. 118:12*. They blaze up fast, make a lot of noise, give out little heat, and soon die out.

"... so is the laughter of the fool: this also is vanity."

The comparison here is between the loud noise and short duration of the music and mirth of fools (V-4) and the short duration of thorns burning.

This is what Job meant in *Job 20:5*, where he says, "That the triumphing of the wicked is SHORT, and the joy of the hypocrite but for a moment." See *Eccl. 2:2*. Then in the Beatitudes of *Luke 6:25* I believe Jesus is referring to the laughter of the world, when he says, "Woe unto ye that are full! for ye shall hunger. Woe unto you that laugh now! for ye shall mourn and weep."

V-7.   *"Surely oppression.maketh a wise man mad;"*

I believe this phrase has a two-fold meaning. This word "oppression" means, unjust of cruel exercise of authority or power, and to burden spiritually or mentally.

1.   It makes a wise man (a just man) angry, to see others mistreated or oppressed. We are told in *Psa. 12:5* that the Lord takes the side of the oppressed. See *Eccl. 5:8* and *Psa. 72:4*. It is the work of the devil to oppress people, but we also know that Jesus came to deliver us from every work of Satan. *Acts 10:38*.

2.   The word "mad," in the bible, means insane, lunatic or crazy. It also means, *completely unrestrained, by reason and judgement*. THEREFORE, if a wise man

98

should engage in oppression of any sort, he has lost his sense of direction, and sound judgement. In *John 10:20*, they accused Jesus of being mad. In *Acts 12:13-16*, Rhoda was accused of being mad, or crazy, when she announced that Peter was standing outside, knocking on the door. Paul was charged with being mad in Acts 26:24-25. See I Cor. 14:23. This type of person needs the faithful rebuke of a wise person.(V-5)

"... *and a gift destroyeth the heart.*"

This phrase makes sense, if we apply the word "gift" to the word bribery. If an otherwise just man looses his sense of direction and engages in "oppression" and bribery, this is another reason for wise rebuke. *Prov. 15:27*. The phrase "destroyeth the heart" corrupts the understanding, takes away wisdom, and we become no better than a fool.

V-8.   "*Better is the end of a thing than the beginning thereof:*"

The word "thing" here can mean any situation we are faced with in this life. It might be physical problems, financial reverses, mental stress and many other things. Regardless of the problem, after we have been through it, we are better able to make a rational judgement, concerning the thing. We might then know the purpose of the problem and whether or not it was advantageous or prosperous for us. How well I remember when we had a church fire. At the beginning, it was hard to see any good in it, but at the end, we were far better off. Jesus made the statement several times in the Gospels, "He that endureth to the end shall be saved." *Matt. 10:22; 22:13*. If we endure to the end of a situation, regardless of how unpleasant, it may be we will have been saved from rash decisions, and possibly loss of rewards, at the Judgement Seat of Christ. *I Cor. 3:12-15*.

"... *and the patient in spirit is better than the proud in spirit.*"

Patience is a virtue that many of us need, in fact, it is one qualification of a bishop or pastor. *I Tim. 3:3; II*

99

Tim. 2:24; and *James4:7-8.* Jesus said in *Luke 21:19,* "In your patience possess ye your souls." I used to pray for patience, until I read *Rom. 5:3* which says, "And not only so, but we glory in tribulations also: knowing that TRIBULATION WORKETH PATIENCE." As for our need of patience see *Heb. 10:36 and 12:1.*

Now concerning the words "proud in spirit", we are told in *Prov. 16:18* that "Pride goeth before destruction, and a haughty spirit before a fall." *Prov. 11:2,* "When pride cometh, then cometh shame: but with the lowly is wisdom." *Heb. 4:6,* "But he giveth more grace. Wherefore he saith, God resisteth the proud, but giveth grace unto the humble." This phrase is repeated in *I Pet. 5:5.*

In the continuation of the contrast of wisdom and folly, we are going to discuss a subject, here in V-9, that connects the two. My prayer to God is that he will give us the discernment to know the difference. We must know how to use anger (for it is not forbidden altogether), but it must be controlled.

V-9.   *"Be not hasty in thy spirit to be angry:"*

Yet we read in *Eph. 4:26,* "Be ye angry and sin not: let not the sun go down upon your wrath." *V-27,* "Neither give place to the devil." Scriptures like these are the reason for Paul's exhortation to Timothy in *II Tim. 2:15.* We must study the Bible in a WORKMAN-LIKE manner, in order to "rightfully divide the word of truth." Anger is an emotional reaction to a certain situation, but does not show intensity or justification. It is sometimes mistaken for wrath, and yet *wrath,* especially on God's part, means "strong vengeful anger," or indignation, and is usually followed by retributory punishment or Divine *chastisement. Heb. 12:6. Rom. 12:19,* "Dearly beloved, avenge not yourselves, but rather give place unto wrath for it is written vengeance is mine; I will repay saith the Lord."

100

Anger can mean the righteous anger of God, or the unrighteous anger of man. V-9 is a warning against the unholy anger of man. *Prov. 14:17* tells us, it makes fools of the person "WHO IS SOON ANGRY" or "always flying off the handle" as we say in the South. We are told in *Prov. 22:24-25*, "Make no friendship with an angry man; and with a furious man thou shalt not go." According to *Prov. 29:22* the unrighteous anger of man stirs up strife.

Col. 3:8 lists, along with anger, some things we are supposed to put off, when we get saved. "But now ye also put off all these; anger, wrath, malice, blasphemy, filthy communication out of your mouth." On the other hand, there is such a thing as righteous indignation, which comes from God, but may also be usurped by men of God. Here are some examples: *Deut. 9:8,20; I Kings 11:9; II Kings 17:18;* and *Psa. 7:11*. There was Aaron in Deuteronomy, Solomon in I Kings, Israel in II Kings, and the wicked in Psalms\

Jesus, himself, showed his indignation in *Matt. 23:33*. After pronouncing all the *WOES* in verses 13-29, he said in *V-33*, "Ye serpents, ye generation of vipers, how can ye escape the damnation of hell." Does anyone think our Lord was in a happy mood, when he uttered these words? OR when he made a whip and ran the moneychangers out of the Temple, in *John 2:13-14?*

There are examples in the Old Testament, of men who got angry at unrighteousness. ENOCH in *Jude 14-15*, MOSES in *Exod. 32:19-20 and Gal. 2:11-14*, where PAUL contended with Peter. Then in *Acts 13:9-11*, where PAUL rebukes Elymas the sorcerer.

A gentle, quiet, reserved character, is to be admired, but should only be half of a person. There are times in our lives when we have to take a stand against evil; and if you think Satan is afraid of our character, you are mistaken. There comes a time, in almost every life, when a little righteous indignation goes a long way. Listen to

Prov. 25:23, "The North wind driveth away rain: so doeth an angry countenance a backbiting tongue."

Every church needs men and women with two sides to their character. They know how to love the good, but they also hate the evil. The kind of gentleness which seeks peace on any terms, has to compromise with sin, and God never allows His people to do that. It is not pleasing to God, nor is it beneficial to man.

We learned that a person who gets angry, suddenly and to often, usually makes a fool of himself. This is especially so if that anger is not controlled by the Holy Spirit. V-10 also has some practical lessons for us. Thus we learn:

V-10. "Say not thou, what is the cause that the former days were better *than these?*

Do you ever long for the "good old days?" Most older saints spend their later years, living in the past. This is not healthy, spiritually speaking. It is also unscriptural; and that is what this verse is all about. Living in the past does nothing to challenge us for the future. This keeps us from being fruitful in old age, which we are told to be in *Psa. 92:14.*

Paul gives us a good recipe, that keeps us from dwelling in the past in *Phil. 3:13-14*. The first thing to do is, "Forgetting those things which are behind." WHY?? Because we cannot bring the past back and relive it. The second ingredient, in this recipe, is "Reaching forth unto those things which are BEFORE." Or, get busy for the future, and you won't have time to live in the past. Regardless of how old we are, ETERNITY is still ahead of us, and it is here and now that we are preparing for it.

In this verse, it seems to me that Solomon was glad he was living in the present, instead of the past. It seems that time has a way of dulling the memory of the past to the extent that we may become completely deluded about the "good old days."

I have, personally, plowed long hours behind a team of horses and mules. Those were some of the "good old days," but the next time I say "get up" to a mule, he is going to be sitting on me.

"... for thou dost not inquire wisely concerning this."

It is better to make the best of the present, and prepare for the FUTURE, than to sit around dreaming about the PAST, since we can not bring it back.

Isa. 42:9 tells us, "Behold, the former things are come to pass, and NEW THINGS DO I DECLARE: before they spring forth I tell you of them." God warned Israel in *Isa. 43:18*, "Remember ye not the former things, (to dwell in the past) neither consider the things of old." for to long for them, would only depress us. We have an example of the children of Israel, comparing the "former days" in *Exod. 16:3* and *Num. 11:5*. Their complaining made Moses angry, which made God angry, and the people felt the wrath of God upon them, for their bellyaching. *Num. 11:10-11.*

V-11.   *"Wisdom is good with an inheritance:"*

This means that having wisdom is as good as having an inheritance. Wisdom will bring good things to those who have it. Remember, we are comparing folly and wisdom, in verses 1-14. To practice those things in verses 9 and 10 is pure folly; on the other hand, wisdom is a precious gift. Wisdom can do things that wealth cannot do. It causes one to trust Christ, who saves the soul. Wealth can not buy that. *Psa. 49:6,7;* and *Isa. 55:1-3.* *WISDOM* drives away ignorance and error from our minds. *WISDOM* can guide us through troublous times. *James 1:5* tells us where to get it.

"... and by it there is profit to them that see the SUN."

That is, the light that wisdom gives. *Prov. 8:10-11,* "Receive my instruction, and not silver; and knowledge RATHER than choice gold." V-11, "For wisdom is better than rubies; and ALL the things that may be desired are not to be compared to it." But you may ask WHAT PROFIT? We answer, "Loving God, serving Christ, walk in the Spirit as Paul said in *Eph. 2:6*, "Sitting together in heavenly places in Christ Jesus."

Eph. 1:3, "Blessed be God and Father of our Lord Jesus Christ, who hath blessed us with ALL spiritual blessings in heavenly places in Christ."

We are still on the subject of wisdom contrasted with folly. The words, *wisdom* and *wise*, are found hundreds of times in the Bible. *Crudens Concordance* tells us, these words are used in Scriptures not only for learning, but for skill in the arts; the instinct of birds and beasts; *discretion*; and *spiritual insight*. This is what every child of God needs.

V-12   *"For wisdom is a defense and money is a defense:"*

Which had you rather have, if you could only have one of the two? I would hope that I would choose wisdom, for there is more power in wisdom than there is in money. That's because wisdom comes from God James 1:5. In Job 28, the subject of wisdom is dealt with. Verses 12 and 20 asks the question, "Where shall wisdom be found? and where is the place of understanding?" Then in verses 13-19 and 21-22 tells us where it is not found.

On the other hand, money, many times, comes from the devil through crime such as drug traffic, fraud, or as *Ezek. 22:27* calls it DISHONEST GAIN. Read verses 26-28, which deals with other types of dishonesty.

When we contrast money and wisdom, wisdom is the better of the two, because there are some things money can't buy. Money can buy pleasure but it cannot buy *happiness* and *Joy*. Money can buy religion, but it cannot buy *Christianity*. Money can buy a house, but it cannot buy a *home*. Money can buy respectability, but it cannot buy *character*. Wealth can do many things for those who possess it, but wisdom can do more. *Prov. 3:13-18* and *Prov. 4:5-13*.

104

"... *but the excellency of knowledge is, that wisdom GIVETH LIFE to them that have it.*"

Prov. 3:18 tells us that, "She is a tree of life to them that lay hold upon her." This implies that wisdom restores what we lost, in the fall of man. It points us to Christ, where it is said of him in *Prov. 8:35*, "For whoso findeth me findeth life, and shall obtain favor with God."

V-13. *"Consider the work of God:"*

This statement, "the work of God,"is also found in chapter *3:11* and chapter *8:17*, and relates to the sovereignty of God; which we need to understand, if we understand the rest of this verse.

When we consider the work of God, we realize that, what God has decreed for all of creation, including man, cannot be changed or altered by man. Man, himself, is a work of God, according to *Gen. 2:7*. We read in *Isa. 64:8*, "But now O Lord, thou art our Father; *we are the clay*, and thou our potter, and we are all the work of thy hand." Read also *Isa. 45:9-12*.

Next, we learn a great truth:

"... *for who can make that straight, which he hath made crooked?*"

This is what we call the OMNIPOTENCE of God, meaning He is ALL power. Job declares this in *Job 12:14*, "Behold, he breaketh down, and it cannot be built again; he shutteth up a man, and there can be no opening." *Isa. 25:2*, "For thou hast made of a city an heap; (Sodom and Gomorrah) of a defensed city a ruin; a palace of strangers to be no city; it shall never be built." Then in *Lam. 3:9*, "He hath enclosed my ways with hewn stone, HE HATH MADE MY PATHS CROOKED."

What would be some of the crooked places, in our lives, that God would make? It may be the CROSS that Jesus told us to take up, in *Matt. 16:24*. He said, "If any man will come after me, let him deny himself, and let him take up his cross, and follow me."

105

I Pet. 4:12 says, "Beloved, think it not strange concerning the fiery trial which is to try you, as though some strange thing happened unto you."

Verses *13-19* applies to ALL Christians everywhere.

We were told back in *Ch. 2:24* and *3:22* that there is nothing wrong with enjoying prosperity, that God sends our way. Solomon said in *2:24*, "This I saw that it was from the hand of God." therefore, it is right that man enjoys the fruits of his labour.

V-14.   *"In the day of prosperity be joyful,"*

This is the last verse dealing with the contrast of folly and wisdom, and here in *V-14*, wisdom is the winner. Wisdom allows us to rejoice and be thankful in the day of prosperity; or when everything is going our way. BUT wisdom also gives God the praise for these joyous times, and if we don't honor God in our prosperity, he can withhold the blessings, and even bring judgement upon us. This happened in *Deut. 28:45-48. I Cor. 10:10-11* tells us, these things that happened to the Israelites, were for our *admonition* (warning).

"... but in the day of adversity consider:"

WHAT??? That we can't live on the mountaintop all the time, and that days of adversity, and the days of prosperity are all in the providence of God. They are both needful for the child of God. This word "consider", is an important Bible word, and means to meditate, to determine, and to remember. In *Job 37:14* God told Job to, "Stand still, and consider the wondrous works of God." We are warned in *Psa. 50:22*, "Now consider this, ye that forget God, LEST I TEAR YOU TO PIECES, and there be none to deliver." We are to consider that the DAY OF ADVERSITY may be a wake-up call from God, to get us to consider our ways. *Hag. 1:5,7*, "Now therefore thus saith the Lord of hosts; consider your ways."

"God also hath set the one over against the other,"

106

It seems to me, that God uses this means to balance our lives; that our lives might be proportionate. Job understood this concept, of God's dealing with man, as his sovereignty, and said in *Job 2:10b*, "WHAT? shall we receive good at the hand of God, and shall we not receive evil? In all this (consideration) did not Job sin with his lips." Even in hard times, we are to give God the glory.Psa. 103:1-4.

"*... to the end that man should find nothing after him.*"

If a person's life was one of all adversity, or all prosperity, he would be prone to predict his future. If his life is a mixture of both, he cannot even predict what tomorrow holds, for this is in the divine providence of God. *James 4:13-14* tells us, "Go to now, ye that say, today or tomorrow we will go into such a city, and continue there a year, and buy and sell, and get gain;" *V-15*, "Whereas ye know not what shall be on the morrow. For what is your life? It is even a vapor, that appeareth for a little time, and then vanisheth away."

Our Lord said in *Matt. 6:34*, "Take therefore no thought for the morrow: for the morrow shall take thought for the things of itself. Sufficient unto the day is the evil thereof."

BUT we can praise God for *I Cor. 2:9*, where Paul said, "But as it is written, eye hath not seen, nor ear heard, neither hath entered into the heart of man, the things which God hath prepared for them that love him."

In truth, ALL of man's experiences, here on earth, does not bring knowledge of life after death. For that knowledge, we rely solely on the inspired Word of God.

Last week we concluded the study of contrasting wisdom and folly, and the many areas, in our lives, where we might confuse the two issues.

V-15. "*All things have I seen in the days of my vanity:*"

It seems that Solomon has taken inventory of his life, and at some point in that life, found it to be empty, unproductive, and vain. We know that his experiences in life were inconsistent, irregular, and sometimes abnormal. The word "vanity" is used throughout Scripture to mean an empty, fruitless, and worthless life.

Often times vanity becomes an idol, in the lives of people, and is worshiped, in place of God. For instance, In *Isa.l:10-16*, God warned His people not to bring Him anymore "vain oblations" (meaningless offerings). In *Matt. 15:17* Jesus denounced the scribes and the Pharisees, calling them hypocrites, in their worship of Him. They worshiped him, but it was in vain.

"... there is a just man that perisheth in his righteousness,"

Our Lord tells us in *Matt. 5:45* that it rains on the just and the unjust alike. This perplexes many people, but the Psalmist enlarges on the idea in *Psa. 73:1-22.*

Good people have to suffer many times in this life, but are promised rewards in the next life. BUT nowhere in the Bible are the wicked promised anything but punishment. Read *I Pet. 2:20; 3:14,17;* and *4:15-19.* Christians have the promise of the Lord in *Rev. 2:10.*

"... and there is a wicked man that prolongeth his life in his wickedness."

This was the perplexing question that David had to settle in *Psa. 73.* We wonder why good men suffer, and wicked men prosper, until we see the whole picture of HERE and HEREAFTER. *Eccl. 8:12-13* is still in the book. This passage in *Eccl. 8* is in contrast with *Deut. 5:33,* where God promises to prolong the lives of his people, and yet warns them in *Deut. 8:17-20.* From these passages we learn that longevity is not always a blessing. Especially if there is suffering involved.

"Be not righteous over much;"

I think we could also say, "Be not over much righteous," or don't be self-righteous. There are many people in this world, that are so heavenly minded, they are no earthly good. *Isa. 64:6* declares that all our righteousness are as filthy rags. Then *Rom. 3"10* says, "As it is written there is none righteous, no not one." In our own stead, we have nothing to offer God, but self with all our sins.

Christians do have righteousness, but we are made righteous through the IMPUTED righteousness of Christ Jesus. Read *Rom. 4:11,22-24.* James, in speaking of Abraham, said in *James 2:23,* "... Abraham believed God, and it was imputed unto him for righteousness: and he was called the Friend of God."

However, when man mixes his self-righteousness with God's imputed righteousness, he becomes OVER MUCH RIGHTEOUS, or too righteous for his own good. these are the people Paul speaks of in *II Cor. 10:12.*
"... neither make thyself over wise:"

The same principle applies to this phrase as the last one. Don't try to out-think God, or you could wind up like the people in *Rom. 1:22* where Paul said, "Professing themselves to be wise, they became fools." *Rom. 11:25,* "Lest ye be wise in your own conceits." Then in *Rom. 12:16b,* "Be not wise in your own conceits."

We are warned in *I Cor. 1:19,* "For it is written, I will destroy the wisdom of the wise (those wise in their own conceits) and will bring to nothing the understanding of the prudent."

I Cor. 3:18-19, Let no man deceive himself. If any man among you seemeth to be wise in this world, let him become a fool, that he may be wise." *V-19,* "For the wisdom of this world is foolishness with God. For it is written, He taketh the wise in their own craftiness." Paul said in *I Cor. 4"10,* "We are FOOLS for Christ's sake." The world saw them as fools.
"... why shouldest thou destroy thyself?"

It seems to me, that the meaning of this phrase is, that when we try and go beyond God's wisdom, and His righteousness, we will SELF DESTRUCT. *Hos. 13:9,* "O Israel, thou hast destroyed thyself; but in me is thine help."

We learned from *V-16*, that to be self-righteous or trying to be wiser than God, causes a person to self-destruct. Now here in *V-17* and *18* the preacher is going to add a few more thoughts to the subject of moderation in wisdom. We have learned from Scriptures like *James 1:5* that TRUE wisdom comes from God, therefore a wise man will:

V-17.   *"Be not over much wicked,"*

This word "wicked" means morally corrupt, very bad, or evil. Webster says it also means, "disgustingly unpleasant."

The Bible has much to say about wickedness. For instance, *Job 21:30* tells us, "That the wicked is reserved to the day of destruction? they shall be brought forth to the day of wrath." *Isa. 57:20-21* tells us they have no peace.

Because of the old nature, there is a certain amount of wickedness in every heart, according to *Jer. 17:9*. But God can and will give us a clean heart, David prayed for this in *Psa. 51:10* and *73:1*. Wickedness is like cancer, it just gets worse, and keeps eating away at the moral fiber of individuals or nations. An illustration of this is seen in *Gen. 6:5*, "And God saw that the wickedness of man was great in the earth." See *Jer. 3:1-2*, and *Hos. 7:2*.

"... neither be thou foolish:"

This word is just a step above wickedness, and is a fore-runner to wickedness if allowed to remain in our lives. Many parents even cultivate foolishness in the hearts of their children. *Prov. 22:15* says, "Foolishness is bound in the heart of a child; but the rod of correction shall drive it far from him." See *Job 5:2-3* and *I Pet. 2:15*.

"... why shouldest thou die before thy time?"

From this question, it seems that to be wicked, or foolish, may cause one's life to be cut short. We have further proof of this in *I Cor. 11:28-32*.

I have personally seen several instances of young people, as well as old people, whose lives were cut short, because of a foolish act (usually disobedience). *Prov. 9:6* says, "Forsake the foolish and live; and go in the way of understanding." *Prov. 10:14,27,* and *Job 22:15-16.*

V-18.　*"It is good that thou shouldest take hold of this;"*

I believe what Solomon means, here in verses 15-18, is that true wisdom gives us the ability to walk that straight and narrow path between two extremes.

On the one hand, there are those who are too hard and self-righteous and bind heavy burdens on others, like the SCRIBES and PHARISEES in the Gospels. Then on the other hand, there are those who are to loose and lax in their morals. The two groups are either too far left, or too far right of what grace teaches. We remember Paul's warning in *II Cor. 10:12.* Grace enables us to walk that straight and narrow path.

"... yea, also from this withdraw not thine hand:"

We should keep a heavy hand upon our ways, and as much as lieth within us, live righteously and Godly in this present world, for none of these verses give the christian the right to sin.

"... for he that feareth God shall come forth of them all."

The word "feareth" here, means a healthy respect for God and His Word. *Psa. 110:10* tells us, "the fear of the Lord is the beginning of wisdom." The person who fears the Lord, will come forth victorious over all extremes and any situation he may encounter in this life.

In the study of wisdom we are told to use caution in dispensing it, lest we make ourselves "over-wise." and self-righteous. The Bible tells us that true wisdom comes from God, and that our wisdom is not to be compared to God's wisdom. *I Cor. 1:19-21.*

V-19.　*"Wisdom strengtheneth the wise more than ten mighty men which are in the city."*

It seems to me that the "wise" mentioned here, is the person who values God's wisdom over his own. God does give wisdom to those who desire it. *James 1:5* and

111

Prov. 2:6. It stands to reason, that if we have the wisdom which comes from God, it puts us on His side, and He is omnipotent (all power).

In *Job 28:12* the question is asked, "But where shall wisdom be found? and where is the place of understanding?" In *Job 33:33* God told Job to keep still and listen and He would teach him wisdom. *Eccl. 7:12* tells us that, "Wisdom is a defense." *Prov. 24:5* says, "A wise man is strong; yea, a man of knowledge increaseth strength." The challenge here is, to pick out the ten strongest men in the city, and they couldn't hold a candle to God's strength. This is what wisdom tells us.

V-20. *"For there is not a just man upon earth, that doeth good, and sinneth not."*

How is this statement related to the previous verse? *Psa. 111:10*, and *Prov. 9:10*, also *Job 28:28* tells us that the fear of the Lord is the beginning of wisdom.

Wisdom reveals man's sinfulness to him, and shows him a way out of the course he has taken.

Respect for God causes a person to see the truth of verse 20, and how helpless man is to affect his own redemption. For instance *Prov. 20:9* asks the question, "Who can say, I have made my heart clean, I am pure from my sin?" Then in *Rom. 3:9-18,23*, Paul exposes mans condition, apart from God. God's wisdom makes a person realize this truth.

V-21. *"Also take no heed unto all words that are spoken;"*

This verse is a warning. Here again, wisdom comes to the rescue, to keep us from hearing many things that would hurt our testimony for Christ. We have an example of this very thing, in the person of Lot. *II Pet. 2:7,8* tells us he vexed his soul with the filthy conversation of the wicked. There are some things we should not listen to such as:

1. Words of a "talebearer" *Lev. 19:16; Prov. 11:13; 18:8; 26:20.*

2. "Backbiting. We read in *Rom. 1:30* that God puts backbiters in the same category as God-haters. Read also *V-24-32* of that same chapter. See also *Psa. 15:1-5; 101:5;* II Cor. 12:19-21. Backbiting and tale-bearing is a sure sign of carnality and worldliness.

"... *lest thou hear thy servant curse thee.*"

You see, there are some things that we don't want to hear about ourselves. The servant would be sure to know his masters faults, but his master would not like to hear them from his servant. This would be one of those times when the truth hurts.

There is a children's song that says,"Be careful little ears what you hear." This is good advice for the big ears as well. This is one meaning of verse 21. "Lest thou hear thy servant curse thee."

V-22.   "*For oftentimes also thine own heart knoweth that thou thyself like- wise hast cursed others.*"

We are discussing the strength of wisdom in Vs.19-29. One of the things wisdom enables us to do, is judge self first.

Paul warns the Corinthians about hasty judgement in *I Cor. 4:5* and *I Cor. 11:31-32.* Our Lord forbids judgement of others, in the Sermon on the Mount in *Matt. 7:1-6.*

When we speak ill of others, we should not get offended when others say harsh things about us; after all, *Gal. 6:7-8* is still in the book. Wisdom protects us from this folly of using self as the standard for judging others. *II Cor. 10:12.*

V-23.   "*All this have I proved by wisdom:*"

God's wisdom, not his own. The Scriptures tell us in *I Kings 4:29-31,* and *V. 34,* that Solomon was the wisest man living, in his day. Jesus Himself, refers to his wisdom in *Matt. 12:42.* The wisdom which God gave Solomon, allowed him to search out all perplexing questions facing man, and answer them, so that we might escape some of the consequences, of otherwise dumb acts. My prayer is that I might have the wisdom of God that would help me to prosper by the mistakes of others. *"I said, I will be wise; but it was far from me."*

Though God had given Solomon all the wisdom he would ever need, it seems he wanted to add some of his own, when he said, "I WILL BE WISE. He found that his own wisdom could not measure up to the wisdom which God gave him.

There is another great man in the O.T. that discovered the truth about God's great wisdom. He explains what he found in Job 28. Read the whole chapter.

The wisdom of God, teaches us of our limitations. It seems to me that Job was not too far behind Solomon, as far as wisdom was concerned.

V-24. *"That which is far off, and exceeding deep, who can find it out?"*

NOT MAN! The preacher has discovered some things about God and creation, that man will never know. Speaking of God's creative acts, *Job 9:10* tells us, "Which doeth great things past finding out; (by man) yea, and wonders without number."

Paul agrees in *Rom. 11:13*, that God's ways are past finding out. This confirms what *Isa. 55:8-9* says about God's ways and thoughts. *I Cor. 1:18-25* describes those who think they have God figured out. Read also *I Cor. 3:18-20*.

Job 11:7-9 poses the question, "Canst thou by searching find out God? or canst thou find out the Almighty unto perfection?" *V-8*, "It is as high as heaven; what canst thou do? deeper than hell; what canst thou know?" *V-9*, "The measure thereof is longer than the earth, and broader than the sea." This is concerning the secrets of wisdom, mentioned in verse 6.

I believe we could truthfully say of Solomon, that he never did anything half-heartedly, but that he put forth all his might, in everything he undertook. As a matter of fact, he encourages us to do the same thing in *Eccl. 9:10*. I believe *Rev. 3:15* bears out this theory of serving God. God said, "I know thy works, that thou art neither cold nor hot: I would that wert cold or hot." ONE OR THE OTHER.

V-25. "*I applied mine heart to know and to search, and to seek out wisdom,*"

It would seem, that the preacher gave up self for this investigation into wisdom. There is a group of people in *Acts 17:11*, in the city of Berea, of whom it is said that they, "Received the word with all readiness of mind, and *searched* the scriptures daily, whether those things were true."

V-12 gives the results of this diligent search of the scriptures. "Therefore many of them believed; also of honorable women which were Greeks (Gentiles) and of men not a few."

Jesus said in *John 5:39*, "Search the scriptures; for in them ye think ye have eternal life: and they are they which testify of me." There was something else Solomon wanted to know:

"*... and the reason of things,*"

God gives us the power to reason, or prove the things of himself. God said to Isaiah in *Isa. 1:18*, "Come now, let us reason together, saith the Lord." That the Sovereign God would REASON with man, flatters man. He also said in *Mal. 3:10*, "And prove me now herewith." (Or put me to the test.) *Heb. 5:14* tells us, "Strong meat belongeth to them that are of full age, even those who by reason of use have their senses exercised to discern BOTH good and evil."

The very reason that many people are always in trouble of one kind or another, is simply because they do not exercise their reasoning power, therefore never learn anything about God. *Heb. 5:13* says plainly, "For everyone that useth milk (I Cor. 3:1-2) is unskillful in the word of righteousness: for he is a babe." Solomon exercised his reasoning power, do we?

"... and to know the wickedness of folly,"

One meaning which Webster gives to the word *"folly"* is; "Lack of good sense or normal prudence and foresight." He also says it means, "A foolish act or idea." Or "an excessively costly or unprofitable undertaking."

Prov. 14:8,18,24,29 shed a lot of light on this word "folly". *Prov. 15:21a* tells us, "Folly is joy to him that is destitute of wisdom." Jeremiah warns about the folly of the prophets in *Jer. 23:13-14*. God will, one day, expose the folly of false teachers according to *II Tim. 3:8-9*.

I Cor. 1:21 tells us, "It pleased God by the foolishness of preaching to save them that believe." BUT he did not say, the preaching of foolishness, or folly.

"... even of foolishness and madness:"

It seems to me that the lack of wisdom, in the service of God, leads to wickedness, folly, foolishness, and finally madness, which is companion to insanity.

Madness means rage, but also means ecstasy, and enthusiasm. *It means frenzied behavior*. The apostle Paul warns about this kind of behavior in *I Cor. 14:23*.

In verse 25, we find Solomon searching for wisdom, and to know the reason of things. It seems to me that the "foolishness and madness" mentioned in V-25, is the reason for the conclusions drawn in the rest of this chapter. In *I Kings 11:1-8* we are given a glimpse of the relationship of this man Solomon with women.

V-26.   *"And I find more bitter than death the woman, whose heart is snares and nets, and her hands as bands:"*

When we look at the problems he had in I Kings 11:1,4,11, we can understand the reason for his conclusion about women. Also when we go back to the beginning of the human race, we remember who the serpent approached first. Beginning with Adam, women have generally wrought havoc in the world. In *Neh. 13:26*, referring to Solomon again, we read,

"Nevertheless even him did outlandish women cause to sin." Then in *Isa. 3:12*, God warns his people about women rulers.

We must understand that Solomon's discovery about women is not a blanket indictment against all women. Only those whose hearts are *snares and nets*, or as *Neh. 13* says, OUTLANDISH.

I am personally convinced that there is nothing more disgusting than an ungodly woman. And I have met a few. BUT, we are reminded that the same man that penned these words, also wrote Proverbs. In the last chapter of that book he extols the virtues of Godly women. Then in *Eccl. 9:9* he applauds a happy marriage. *"... whoso pleaseth God shall escape her;"*

In the wisdom that God gives, there is discretion and discernment. The person who has these attributes will make the right choices, usually.

The choosing of a life-mate should be the most important addition to our life, after salvation. *"... but the sinner shall be taken by her."*

The lost person is only motivated by the LUST of the flesh, the LUST of the eyes, and by the PRIDE of life, and is usually incapable of making the right choice; though some of us do luck out and choose a good woman for life.

V-27. *"Behold this have I found, saith the preacher, counting one by one, to find the account."*

In the beginning of this book in *Ch. 1:1-2*, the preacher said, "Vanity of vanities; all is vanity." He repeated this phrase in the last chapter (12:8).

The phrase "counting one by one" means, he has observed women and men and examined their character and conduct. He has come to these conclusions through his own observations. He means he has weighed one thing against another to find the reason of things.

V-28. *"Which yet my soul seeketh, but I find not:"*

117

He said in V-25, "I applied mine heart to know, and to search, and to seek out wisdom, and to know the reason of things." In my opinion, Solomon is searching for the deep rooted reason why women are so different from men in their very nature. AFTER ALL, Eve was taken from Adam's side. It would seem, Solomon's search was in vain, for he said "I find not." (the answer). He examined a thousand men and found ONE. This phrase is also found in *Job 33:23*, "One among a thousand," (who are upright). The odds were even greater than this in Noah's day. Only eight people in the whole world.

"*... but a woman among all those have I not found.*"

Remember, he had had experience with 700 wives and 300 concubines, which were secondary wives; and usually purchased slaves. He has had experience with one thousand women when he wrote these words. Solomon is not condemning all women, for he said in *Prov. 12:4*, "A virtuous woman is a crown to her husband, but she that maketh ashamed is as rottenness in his bones." Then in *Prov. 31:10-33* he lists the attributes of a virtuous woman.

V-29. "*Lo, this only have I found, that God hath made man upright;*"

Here, we are taken back to the original creation, when man came from the hands of the creator. *Gen. 1:26-31.* Solomon is saying, in effect, here in Ecclesiastes, that we can't blame God for man's downfall. Man has sought many ways, and even invented a few, to disobey his Creator.

Chapter 8

In chapter seven we discussed "wisdom" in several aspects. We saw wisdom and folly contrasted; along with the importance of moderation, in the use of wisdom, lest we make ourselves "over-much wise." V-16. Finally the strength of wisdom. Now, here in the first part of chapter 8, we are told to recognize and submit to those in authority.

V-1. *"Who is a wise man? and who knoweth the interpretation of a thing?"*

Two important questions:

1. Who is a wise man? Who determines if he is indeed wise? The quest for wisdom started back in *Gen. 3:6* with Eve, in the garden of Eden. But she abused it, like the serpent knew she would. *Job 5:13* and *I Cor. 3:19* both tell us that man's wisdom, apart from God, trips him up. "He taketh the wise (wiseacre) in their own craftiness." In *I Cor. 1:19* and *Isa. 29:14* the Bible tells us the wisdom of man will perish. Listen to *Prov. 26:12*, where it says, "Seest thou a man who is wise in his own conceit? there is more hope of a fool than of him." BUT Prov. 28:7 tells us, "Whoso keepeth the law is a wise son." (the law of his father) Some are wise to do evil, *Jer. 4:22*. Some are wise to do good, *Prov. 11:30*, "He that winneth souls is wise."

2. Who knows how to interpret anything? This means who has the gift of discernment, to explain dreams and visions and to know the difference between the two. We have an example of interpreting dreams and visions in *Gen. 40:8-13*, in the person of Joseph. His ability came from God. In other words, he did not give his own private interpretation of the dream.

We are told in *II Pet. 1:20* that the Scriptures are of no PRIVATE interpretation. This means the Word of God does not have one meaning for the Baptists, another for the Catholics, and yet another for the Methodists and Charismatics.

We have another illustration of discernment in the book of Daniel. In *Dan. 5:10-29*, Daniel was called in to interpret a dream for Belshazzar, even though it was BAD news for Mr. Belshazzar. V-30. Another example is found in *Dan. 4:19-27* where Daniel unraveled a mystery for King Nebuchadnezzar. Again he did not like what he heard. We understand Daniel to be a man of great courage. Even when facing kings, he told it like it was.

We are told in *II Tim. 2:15* to rightly divide the WORD OF TRUTH. To do so, takes both discernment and holy-boldness, or courage. We are warned by our Lord in *John 5:39* and *Matt. 22:29.*
"... a man's wisdom maketh his face to shine and the boldness of his face shall be changed."

A man or woman whom God has given wisdom, displays a cheerful countenance. They either know the answer to every problem they face, or they know who has the answer; therefore they wear a happy expression on their face. This type of person never goes around wearing an expression of gloom and doom.

What Solomon is saying here is that if we have that inner light, that inward glow, it will be reflected in our outward appearance. This is what Jesus meant in *Matt. 5:14-16.* This type of Christian looks at the world with assurance and confidence. He can do all things through Christ, who strengthens him. *Phil. 4:13, 19 and II Tim. 1:12.*

We are still on the subject of submission to authority, which is very important to the child of God. In *I Chron. 29:24* we have an illustration of the subjects of King David, transferring their allegiance to Solomon when he became king.

V-2.   *"I counsel thee to keep the kings commandment,"*

This is one of the answers to the question in verse one, "Who is a wise man?" A wise man will recognize authority and honor it.

Heb. 13:17 tells us to, "Obey them that have the rule over you, and submit yourselves: for they watch for your souls, as they that must give account, that they may do it with joy, and not with grief (to you) for that is unprofitable for you."

One of the cardinal teachings of the word of God is obedience. *Eph. 6. 1* "Children obey your parents in the Lord: for this is right."

Col. 2:20, "Children obey your parents in all things."

Col. 2:22, "Servants obey in all things your masters according to the flesh." *Titus 3:1*, "Put them in mind to be subject to principalities and powers, to obey magistrates, to be ready to every good work." We are told in *I Sam. 15:22* that, "To obey is better than sacrifice."

Read Rom. 13:1-7; Jer. 7:23-24; 11:4, 7-8.

"... and that in regard of the oath of God."

An oath is a solemn appeal to God to witness the truth of a declaration. Meaning that if you invoke God's name into an oath, it is doubly binding. But an oath may also be made without invoking Deity. We have an illustration in *II Chron. 36:11-14* of King Zedekiah, who broke the oath that Nebuchadnezzar made him take before God. Because of this, he led his people into much sin.

V-3.   *"Be not hasty to go out of his sight:"* (the kings)

Cain went out from the presence of the Lord, and dwelt in the land of Nod (means wandering). Cain's new place of residence was brought on because he killed his brother Abel. The king watches over and provides for his subjects, just as God cares for His children, therefore we are to walk circumspectly before God and the world.

"... stand not in an evil thing;"

121

Paul tells us in *I Thess. 5:22* to, "Abstain from all appearance of evil" *I Thess. 4:3* says to, "Abstain from fornication."

Finally, *I Pet. 2:11*, "Dearly beloved, I beseech you as strangers and pilgrims ABSTAIN from fleshly lusts, which war against the soul."

"... *for he (the king) doeth whatsoever pleaseth him.*"

Even though the king is sovereign he may also be evil, and can cause his subjects much grief.

Prov. 20:2 says, "The fear of a king is as the roaring of a lion: whoso provoketh him to anger sinneth against his own soul." Or brings problems upon himself.

We are still on the subject of submission to authority. Solomon is using the earthly king as an example of Sovereignty. I believe when we as believers, put God in the place of the king, and self as subjects, we will enjoy the blessing of God upon our lives.

V-4.   "*Where the word of a king is, there is power:*"

Notice that the king does not have to be there in person, just his word. It should be the same with the WORD of GOD, for the christian. There is power in the kings word, because he is sovereign and there is no one else to appeal to. We have an illustration of a kings power in *Dan. 3:2*, in the person of Nebuchadnezzar. He passed the word and all classes of people obeyed his word. Wouldn't it be great if all believers were that obedient to the commands of Christ. After all he said in *Matt. 28:18*, "ALL power is given unto me in heaven and in earth"

"... *and who may say unto him, What doest thou?*"

Who is going to question the king's authority? In Job 9:12 the same question is asked of God, the sovereign of the universe, "Behold, he taketh away, who can hinder him? who will say unto him (God) what doest thou?" See also *Job 9:13-14* and *Dan. 4:34-37*.

122

Nebuchadnezzar finally woke up and confessed that there was a higher power than himself. If puny man would just get this through his head, the world would be a far better place to live in. *Isa. 45:9.*

V-5.　*"Whoso keepeth the commandment shall feel no evil thing:"*

This should encourage obedience in God's children. Compare *Prov. 24:21-22* and *Rom. 13:1-7.*

"... and a wise man's heart discerneth both time and judgement."

I believe what Koheleth is saying here is, that a wise man knows both the time to obey God's word, and the judgement for not doing so. According to *Eccl. 12:14*, the wise man knows there is coming a time when "God shall bring every work into judgement, with every secret thing, whether it be good, or whether it be evil."

V-6.　*"Because to every purpose there is time and judgement, therefore the misery of man is great upon him."*

According to *Eccl. 3:1,17; and Eccl. 6:1* everything has an appointed time of duration. Paul said in *Rom. 3:16*, speaking of man in general, "Destruction and misery are in their ways." V-17, "And the way of peace have they not known." V-18, "There is no fear of God before their eyes." Yet we learn from the Scriptures, that God is grieved when his people are miserable. *Judges 10:16*, "And they put away the strange gods from among them, and served the Lord: and his (God's) soul was grieved for the misery of Israel."

Verses five and six are referring to time and judgement, and we believe the seventh verse is a follow up of the same subject.

V-7.　*"For he knoweth not that which shall be:"* Meaning, we don't know how light or severe the judgement might be, nor do we know when the judgement will come. BUT, for disobedience, it will come, for we are warned in *Prov. 24:22*, "For their calamity shall rise suddenly; and who knoweth the ruin of them both?"

"... for who can tell him when it shall be?"

The disobedient person knows not how retribution will come, nor can anyone else enlighten him. It is in the hands of a sovereign God or king. *Deut. 32:4,41* tells us, "He is the rock, his work is perfect: for all his ways are judgement:A God of truth and without iniquity, just and right is he." V-41, "If I whet my glittering sword, and mine hand take hold on judgement; I will render vengeance to mine enemies, and will reward them that hate me."

We are warned in *Eccl. 12:14* that, "God shall bring every work into judgement, with every secret thing, whether it be good, or whether it be evil."

V-8. *"There is no man that hath power over the spirit to retain the spirit;"*

Even though the word "spirit" is not capitalized here, I believe Solomon is referring to the power of God. For instance, in the O.T. There are several places where the word is NOT capitalized, but is referring to God as a power or force, instead of a person. *Gen. 1:2, Gen. 41:38; I Sam. 10:10; 11:6.* In the New Testament, the word "spirit" is almost always capitalized, because it is referring to the Divine third Person of the Godhead.

IF we make "spirit" to mean the breath of life, this clause makes sense; for the mightiest of men, has not power to prolong life, when the call of death comes.

"... neither hath he power in (or over) the day of death:"

This clause more clearly identifies the previous one, as to subject matter. The preacher is talking about life and death, of which only God holds the key.

"... and there is no discharge in that war:"

The war of life and death. Death is a battle that is fought by every living soul, and yet *Heb. 9:27* says, "And as it is appointed unto men once to die, and after this the judgement." There is no substitution here, for we cannot get someone else to die for us. Jesus was the only one who ever died in someone else's place. He died a substitutionary death for all mankind.

We are told in *Psa. 49:6-7* that wealth does not keep men from dying. On the other hand, the person whose trust is in the Lord, has these promises in *Psa. 34:7,8,15,17.*
"... neither shall wickedness deliver those that are given to it."

Psa. 52:7 is a warning to all, "Lo, this is the man that made NOT God his strength; (sounds like the New Age movement to me) but trusted in the abundance of his riches, and strengthened himself in his wickedness." *BUT*, remember *Gen. 6:5* where God saw the wickedness of man and knew exactly how to stop it, although he used drastic measures. *Job 4:8* says, "Even as I have seen, they that plow iniquity, and sow wickedness, REAP THE SAME."

Job 11:11, "For he knoweth vain men: he seeth wickedness also; will he not then consider it?"

Verse nine ends the subject of submission to authority, that we have been discussing since verse one.

V-9.　　*"All this have I seen, and applied my heart unto every work that is done under the sun:"*

Solomon, having been a ruler himself, had observed man in every situation pertaining to life under the sun; from rulers to the ruled; from the lowest to the highest of society.

He said he applied his heart. To do that, he had to be submissive to the discipline of the mind, in order to realize the objective of understanding humanity. He said in *Eccl. 7:23*, "All this have I proved by wisdom." Here again, he was in submission to the wisdom of God. He had to give up his own wisdom, for he said in this verse, "I said I will be wise; but it was far from me." In other words, he learned from God not himself.

125

"... there is a time wherein one man ruleth over another to his own hurt."

Meaning the ruler is hurt more than the ruled because; absolute power corrupts absolutely. I don't know who said that, but it is true nevertheless. Also in the case of a despot (tyrant who abuses his authority). The one who is under him is abused. In *Eph. 6:12* Paul said, "For we wrestle not against flesh and blood, but against principalities, against powers, against the *rulers of darkness* of this world, against spiritual wickedness in high places."

God did not intend it to be that way, for he says in *Rom. 13:3*, "For rulers are not a terror to good works, but to the evil. Wilt thou then not be afraid of the power? do that which is good, and thou shalt have praise of the same." (Good works).

Gal. 6:7 is still in the book.

In the rest of chapter eight, verses 10-17, we are going to discuss the fact that finite man cannot understand all the works of a infinite God.

V-10. *"And so I saw the wicked buried,"*

The one who ruled to his own hurt. He may have prospered while he was in power, and reached the height of success, but he is dead now. *Eccl. 9:4* tells us, "For to him that is joined to all the living there is hope: for a living dog is better than a dead lion." The law of sowing and reaping, and the law of retribution works on the rulers as well as the subjects they rule.

In *Luke 16:22* the rich man died and was buried (possibly in pomp and splendor). BUT verse 23 says, "And in HELL he lifted up his eyes." His money and power could do him no good, on the other side of death. For the evil person (even kings or rulers), *Isa. 14:9* tells us, "Hell from beneath is moved for thee to meet thee at thy coming: it stirreth up the dead for thee (what a welcoming committee) even all the chief ones of the earth."

126

V-11, "Thy pomp is brought down to the grave."
"... *who had come and gone from the place of the holy,
AND WERE FORGOTTEN IN THE CITY where they
had so done: this also is vanity.*"

They were EMPTY AND VAIN. Their success in
life, could not keep them from dying and returning to
dust, like any other mortal being. In *Psa. 49:16-20*, the
Psalmist tells us not to be afraid of the rich and famous,
for they don't take their fame and power with them,
when they leave this world for the next.

One of the reasons that man fails to understand the workings
of a Holy God is because when we sin, God does not bring judgement upon us at that very moment. Man thinks that God did not
see him, or that he was just to busy to notice. Therefore, man
thinks he is getting away with sin. This is the meaning of verse 11.

V-11. "Because sentence against an evil work is not executed
speedily," *Psa. 10:11* says it best, when it says of man,
"He hath said in his heart, God hath forgotten: he hideth
his face; he will never see it." Man presumes upon God's
mercy and longsuffering, but *II Pet. 3:9* warns against
the sin of presumption. In *Psa. 19:13* David prayed,
"Keep back thy servant also from presumptuous sins; let
them not have dominion over me: then shall I be upright,
and I shall be innocent of the great transgression."

Peter tells us in *II Pet. 2:10* those who "Walk after
the flesh in the lust of uncleanness" are *presumptuous.*

When man thinks he is getting away with sin, he is
deceiving himself. *Num. 32:23* tells us, "Be sure your
sin will find you out."
"... *therefore the heart of the sons of men is fully set in
them to do evil.*" See *Eccl. 9:3.*

The word "heart" as used in the scriptures, means the
mental intellect of man. His mind, his emotions, (which
causes action) as well as the organ which pumps the
blood through the body. *Jer. 17:9* gives God's description

of the heart. He said, "The heart is deceitful *above all things*, and desperately wicked: who can know it?"

Our Lord gives a discourse on the heart, in *Matt. 15:18-20.* He said in V-18, "But those things which proceed out of the mouth come from the heart; and they defile the man." V-19, "For out of the heart proceed evil thoughts, murders, adulteries, fornications, thefts, false witness, blasphemies." V-20, "these are the things which defile a man: but to eat with unwashed hands defileth not a man."

V-12.   *"Though a sinner do evil a hundred times,"*

In other words, he sins continually and thinks he is immune from the chastening hand of God. *Isa. 65:20b* tells us, "But the sinner being an hundred years old shall be accursed."

We learn that age is no insurance against the judgement of a just God. It is a true saying, "There is no fool like an old fool."

In *Job 32:9*, God said, "Great men are not always wise; neither do the aged understand judgement."

See Paul's teaching of the aged in *Tit. 2:1-4*

"... and his days are prolonged, yet surely I know that it shall be well with them that fear God, which fear before him."

He may live to be a ripe old age, but if he dies a sinner, his longevity has availed nothing in his behalf. He still has to face a just and righteous God.

On the other hand, they who live long and productive lives, in fear and respect for God, shall be blessed with untold blessings. *Mal. 3:16-18* tells of the faithful remnant, and V-16 says, "Then they that feared the Lord spake often to one another." Meaning they encouraged one another.

In verses 12-13 Solomon is contrasting those who fear, or have a healthy respect for God, with those who are wicked and have no fear of God.

V-13.   *"But it shall not be well with the wicked."*

    The word "wicked" means morally corrupt. evil, and a very bad person likely to come to harm, distress and trouble. *Prov. 10:30* tells us, there is coming a time when the wicked will not inherit the earth. "The righteous shall never be moved: but the wicked shall not inhabit the earth." For this reason, we preachers are duty-bound to warn the wicked of their ungodly ways. *Ezek. 3:18-19; 33:8-9.* Because there is hope for the wicked if he turns from his wickedness. *Ezek. 18:21-23.*

"... neither shall he prolong his days, which are as a shadow;

    Job 14:2 tells us, "He (man) cometh forth like a flower, and is cut down: he fleeth also as a shadow, and continueth not.

    Job 8:9, "For we are but yesterday, (history) and know nothing, because our days upon earth are a shadow."

    Job 14:5, "Man's life is like a shadow; fleeting and soon passing."

V-14.   *"There is a vanity which is done upon the earth:"*

    Here, I believe, Solomon is referring to the seeming injustice found in the following statements. When we first think of how evil men seem to prosper, and righteous people sometime suffer, we are prone to question, and even blame God; so this vanity is from man's point of view. It seems vain to mortal man.

    Psa. 37:1-2 tells us not to be envious of the evil doers. In fact, the entire 73rd Psalm deals with the destiny of the just and the unjust. When we understand their end, it is foolish to envy them in this life.

"... that there be just men, unto whom it happeneth according to the work of the wicked."

    We are told in *Matt. 5:45*, "That ye may be the children of your Father which is in heaven: for he maketh his sun to rise on the evil and on the good, and sendeth rain on the just and on the unjust."

Read *Psa. 37:7-17.*

"... *again, there be wicked men, to whom it happeneth according to the work of the righteous:*"

Some people have the mistaken idea that all who are saved should be wealthy, but this just isn't so. Not everyone can handle wealth and prosperity. God certainly knows who can and who cannot. Jesus said in *Matt. 19:24*, "And again I say unto you, it is easier for a camel to go through the eye of a needle, than for a rich man to enter into the kingdom of God."

Jesus had much to say concerning the poor. *Matt;11:5; Matt. 26:11;* and *James 2:5.* If God made everyone wealthy who professed to be a Christian, you probably wouldn't be able to find a lost person anywhere. But they would be saved for the wrong reasons.

Even though we do not understand it now, God will, one day balance the scales of justice, including wealth. Suffice to say now, that God's ways are past finding out.

Rom. 11:33, "O the depth of the riches both of the wisdom and knowledge of God! how unsearchable are his judgements, and his ways past finding out."

When Christians see the prosperity of the wicked, they sometime get discouraged and even envious. The preacher here in our text, recommends mirth as an antidote for these attitudes of God's people.

V-15. *"Then I commended mirth,"*

This word "commend" also means recommend, and here as in other places Solomon recommends laughter or joy, instead of those hurtful emotions of envy and jealousy. The word "mirth" means merriment, or joyfulness and happiness. It is encouraged elsewhere in scriptures. *Pro. 15:13,15, 17:22.* In *James 5:13* we are told, "Is any merry? let him sing psalms." Now we know that merriment may also be sinful and may sometime affect Christians, because Satan cannot stand to see God's people enjoying themselves. The average worldly crowd thinks they have to have booze in order to have a good time, but the more alcohol they consume, the wilder the party gets. This is the reason for scriptures like *Pro. 20:1* that tells us, "Wine is a mocker, strong drink is raging; and whosoever is deceived thereby is not wise."

"*... because a man hath no better thing under the sun, than to eat, and to drink, and to be merry:*"

This concept, of man enjoying the fruits of his labour, is found in several places in the Bible, but is found about six times in Ecclesiastes *2:24; 3:12,22; 5:18; 8:15 and 9:7.* A living, vibrant faith in Jesus Christ will enable us to make the best of every situation we are faced with, and this pleases God. Paul gives us the recipe for happiness in *Phil. 4:11* where he said, "Not that I speak in respect of want: for I have learned, in whatsoever state I am, therewith to be content."

Paul is not talking about a geographical location, but circumstances and situations he is faced with.

"*... for that (attitude of merriment or mirth) shall abide with him of his labour the days of his life, which God giveth him under the sun.*"

The bottom line is, that eating, drinking, and being happy is all that God intended for us to get out of life under the sun, or here on earth. But thank God, we have hope of mansions in eternity, according to *John 14:2.* Jesus said it and I believe it. I believe that throughout eternity, heaven will be filled with joyful surprises. *I Cor. 2:9*

V-16.   "*When I applied mine heart to know wisdom, and to see the business that is done upon the earth:*"

He said in *Ch. 1:13*, "I gave my heart to seek and search out by wisdom concerning all things that are done under heaven." Then in *Ch. 1:16* he reached that goal. Solomon's first and great desire was to know the wisdom of God, and next, to understand the doings of man in every station of life, and to know the end result of his actions here on earth.

"... (for also there is that neither day nor night seeth sleep with his eyes:)"

What he learned was, that there was a restlessness among men, day and night, that caused sleeplessness.

V-17.   "Then I beheld all the work of God, that a man cannot find out the work that is done under the sun:"

His final conclusion, after comparing the works of man with the works of God, was that there was no comparison. He could not understand all the doings of man, let alone the workings of God. *Ch. 3:11*.

"... because though a man labour to seek it out, yet HE SHALL NOT FIND IT;" Chapter 7:23-24; I Cor. 1:20-21.

"... yea further, though a wise man think to know it, YET HE SHALL NOT BE ABLE TO FIND IT."

When Solomon faces these facts about God, that his ways are past finding out, he seems overwhelmed by the immensity of it all. Paul also stood in AWE of God, when he said in *Rom. 11:33*, "O the depth of the riches both of the wisdom and knowledge of God! how unsearchable are his judgements, and his ways past finding out."

Dan. 4:35, "And all inhabitants of the earth are reputed as nothing: and he doeth according to his will in the army of heaven, and among the inhabitants of the earth: and none can stay his hand, or say unto him, what doest thou."

Chapter 9

Although man is unable to understand all of the workings of an Infinite Sovereign God, there is one very important truth about God that all men can understand, and that is, that God will judge every person born since creation. *Heb. 9:27.*

V-1.   *"For all this I considered in my heart even to declare all this,"*

When Solomon beheld all the works of God, and found that he could not understand them, he had to declare this fact to the world, but at the same time; he passes on all the workings of God, that he does understand. There are several in the next few verses.

"... that the righteous, and the wise, and their works, are in the hand of God:"

Alexander Cruden says the word "work" means, "For any thought, word, or outward action, whether good or evil." *Eccl. 12:14* bears this out. We are not discussing the works of God, here in this verse, for they are too great, and too many to even compare with the works of men, which only are in view here. In *Num. 16:28* Moses said, "Hereby ye shall know that the Lord hath sent me to do all these works; for I have NOT done them of myself."

We may take courage from the fact that every work done here on earth, or, "under the sun" that glorifies the Divine Godhead will NOT go unnoticed nor unrewarded. *Prov. 31:31* speaking of a virtuous woman, God said, "Give her the fruit of her hands; and let her own works praise her in the gates."

Rev. 14:13 says, "And I heard a voice from heaven saying unto me, Write, Blessed are the dead which *die in the Lord* from henceforth: Yea, saith the Spirit, that they may rest from their labours: and their works do follow them."

"... *no man knoweth either love or hatred by all that is before them.*"

The emotions of love and hate are not learned through good works. We are not to judge God's love or hatred or what God thinks of the works of others. In other words, we are not to engage in second-guessing God. Because great calamity comes to others, we dare not judge them to be great sinners. We have the illustration of a man born blind, in *John 9:1-3*. We cannot know God's pleasure or displeasure with others. It is hard enough to know his feelings toward our own works. In fact, it may take years before we know whether God was pleased or displeased with some of our works. With many of our works, we will not know how God viewed them, until the judgement seat of Christ. IT IS A GOOD THING THAT GOD DOES NOT TREAT OTHERS AS WE THINK HE OUGHT TO.

We can rest, assured in the fact, that every work of man will be judged by the just and righteous judge. *Rom. 14:10 and I Cor. 3:13-15*. We also have this consolation that God does not forget our works, whether good or bad. *Heb. 6:10* tells us, "For God is not unrighteous to forget your work and labour of love, which ye have shewed toward his name, in that ye have ministered to the saints, and do minister."

V-2.　　*"All things come alike to all:"*

Meaning, with God there is equal justice, and when speaking of judgement, God is no respecter of persons. *Acts 10:34* and *Rom. 2:11*. It may be that these were some of the things that the preacher could not understand about God. It rains on the just and the unjust as Jesus said in *Matt. 5:45*, "That ye may be the children of your Father which is in heaven: for he maketh the sun to rise on the evil and the good, and sendeth rain on the just and the unjust."

V-2.   In continuing with the phrase "All things come alike to all" we understand it to mean, that in judgement and in the providence of God, there is no respect of persons.

"... *there is one event to the righteous, and to the wicked;*"

If verse two teaches anything, it is that God is sovereign. In his Divine Providence, he works everything according to his will. *Rom. 9:6-21* deals specifically with the sovereignty of God. We may be assured of one thing, that nothing is by chance with God. We learned this truth in *Eccl. 3:1-9.*

"... *to the good and to the clean, and to the unclean;*"

Some Christians have trouble understanding this concept of God, as Asaph had in *Psa. 73:3,12,13,17.* The good and clean are those who are cleansed by the blood of Christ. *I John 1:7; Rev. 1:5; 7:14* as well as *I Cor. 6:11.* This is cleansing of the soul, but the cleansing of the walk of the believer is through the Word of God. *Psa. 119:9* and *John 15:3.*

The "unclean" are those who have never trusted Jesus Christ for salvation. The Bible does distinguish between the two. *Isa. 35:8, Ezek. 44:23, Eph. 5:5, and I Thess. 4:7.*

Though our God is Sovereign, he still distinguishes between the saved and the unsaved, between the clean and the unclean. He will one day separate the two classes. Here in verse two, distinctions are made clear.

"... *to him that sacrificeth, and to him that sacrificeth not:*"

This phrase has reference to the outward appearance of religion which our Lord condemns in *Matt. 23:25-28.* Sacrifices started with Cain and Abel, and man has been making them ever since. *Heb. 11:4.* We know that in the Old Testament God recognized certain sacrifices made by his people. For instance, Moses and his followers made sacrifices unto God. *Exod. 3:18; 5:3,8; 8:27; 10:25* and many other scriptures. However, in the dispensation of grace, Christ Jesus made one supreme sacrifice for all time, and for all who would accept that sacrifice for salvation. *Heb. 7:27; 9:26; 10:5,8,12.* Is there any sacrifice that we can make? Yes! *Heb. 13:15-16.*

"... as is the good, so is the sinner;"

Here, again, this phrase refers only to the providence of God in his capacity to direct the destiny of man. For he knows the end of all men. Period!

"... and he that sweareth, as he that feareth an oath."

He that sweareth is the person who takes an oath, or promise to God, lightly or falsely. We are warned in *Ecc1. 5:4* about taking vows too lightly or refusing to keep them. *Num. 30:1-2.,* "And Moses spake unto the heads of the tribes concerning the children of Israel, saying, this is the thing which the Lord hath commanded." *V-2.,* "If a man vow a vow unto the Lord, or swear an oath to bind his soul with a bond; he shall not break his word, he shall do according to all that proceedeth out of his mouth."

Jonah learned the hard way about making and breaking vows to God. He was in the fishes belly when he remembered his broken vow. Read *Jonah 2:9.*

The one event, mentioned in verses one and two, we understand to mean "death." It comes to the rich and famous as well as the common man. Death is man's worst enemy, and though it may be prolonged for awhile, it is inevitable for all the human race. We each have an appointment with the grim reaper.

V-3.   *"This is an evil among all things that are done under the sun,"*

I believe Solomon is saying that all things we have to face, here on earth, death holds the greatest fear. From the Bible we learn that death is the product, and the end result of sin. God told Adam in *Gen. 2:17*, that the day he ate of the forbidden tree, he would die. *Ezek. 18:4,20* tells us, "The soul that sinneth it shall die."

Rom. 5:12 tells us it started with Adam. Then *Rom. 6:23* says, "For the wages of sin is death; but the gift of God is eternal life through Jesus Christ our Lord."

"*... that there is one event unto all:*"

There is no need to elaborate further on that statement.

"*Yea, also the heart of the sons of men is full of evil,*"

Jer. 17:9 describes the heart thusly, "The heart is deceitful above all things, and desperately wicked: who can know it?" But THANK GOD for verse 10 which says,"I the Lord search the heart, I try the reins, even to give every man according to his ways, and according to the fruit of his doings." Basically, man has not changed from the condition found in *Gen. 6:5* and it's only after God performs the world's greatest heart transplant (*Ezek. 36:26-27*), that man is considered good at all.

Prov. 19:21 tells us, "There are many devices in a man's heart; nevertheless the counsel of the Lord, that shall stand."

"*... and madness (wickedness) is in their heart while they live,*"

In Eccl. 1:17 and 2:12, Solomon links madness with folly, and says it causes vexation of the spirit. In *Luke 6:11* we find Jesus healing on the Sabbath, and it caused madness in the hearts of some who witnessed the miracle. Then finally, *I John 5:19* has something to say about a mad world. John said, "And we know that we are of God, and the whole world lieth in wickedness."

"*... and after that they go to the dead.*"

That is, we all go to the place of the dead, or the grave. We are also told in the Scriptures that our WORKS follow us, whether they are GOOD works or BAD works. *II Cor. 5:10.*

For the lost person, their works follow them to the Great White Throne judgement. *Rev. 20:11-12.* In *Rev. 18:6*, referring to Babylon the great, God said he would reward her DOUBLE according to her works, and V-8 defines the plagues that befall her.

V-4.　　*"For to him that is joined to all the living there is hope:"*

As long as there is life, there is hope for change of heart, for the wicked. We believe there is such a thing as death-bed repentance, but that is dangerous to wait for it. There is proof of this idea of salvation at the last minute, in the salvation of one of the thieves who died on the cross beside our Lord. *Matt. 27:44* calls them thieves and *Luke 23:39-43* tells of the salvation of the one who called on the name of the Lord.

"... for a living dog is better than a dead lion."

The lion, in the scriptures, is known for his boldness, *Prov. 28:1* and for his strength in *Prov. 30:30*. Regardless of these attributes, when he is dead, he is nothing.

On the other hand, the dog is not rated very highly, in the Bible. In fact, they are listed in the last chapter of Revelation (*22:15*) and linked with an unwholesome crowd.

Rev. 22:15, "For without are dogs, and sorcerers, and whoremongers, and murderers, and idolaters, and whatsoever liveth and maketh a lie."

V-5.　　*"For the living know that they shall die:"*

Though the way some people live, you would think the subject of death never crosses their mind. The worst thing a person can do in this life is, neglect the subject of death. In neglecting the fact of death, he is not prepared to face eternity. It is only in this life, that we prepare for death. We find in *Amos 4:12* that God told Israel to, "Prepare to meet thy God, O Israel."

Because of the uncertainty of death, it is incumbent upon every individual to prepare for eternity. We know that heaven is a prepared place for a prepared people, and that hell is a prepared place for unprepared people.

"... but the dead know not anything,"

They have severed all ties with life under the sun. Their labor is ended, their physical emotions have

138

ceased. *Job 14:21* verifies this, He said. "His sons come to honor, and he knoweth it not; they arc brought low, but he preceiveth it not of them."

"*... neither have they anymore a reward;*"

From this phrase, we know the preacher is referring to the lost person. The only rewards the unregenerate will ever receive is here on earth, during his life under the sun. For this reason, Paul said in *I Cor. 15:19*, "If in this life only we have hope in Christ, we are of all men most miserable."

Prov. 24:20 says, "For there shall be no reward for the EVIL man; the candle of the wicked shall be put out."

In Matt. 6:1,2,5,16, Jesus talks about a class of people in which the ONLY rewards they will receive is the praise of men.

BUT in contrast, the-righteous are promised rewards throughout the Scriptures. The Psalmist said in *Psa. 112:6b*, "... the righteous shall be in everlasting remembrance."

Psa. 58:11 "So that man shall say, Verily there is a reward for the righteous: verily he is a God that judgeth in the earth."

Prov. 11:18. "The wicked worketh a deceitful work: but to him that soweth righteousness shall be a sure reward."

In *Matt. 10:41-42* our Lord promised rewards, and in several of Paul's letters, rewards are promised.

Concerning promised rewards, see *I Cor. 3:8,14; Col. 3:24; I Tim. 5:18; Rev. 11:18-* and *Rev. 22:12.*

"*... for the memory of them (the lost) is forgotten.*"

Forgotten only so far as man is concerned, for we know that God does not forget the works of the lost person. Their names are found in the books, mentioned in *Rev. 20:11-15 and Psa. 109:14-15.*

V-6. Verse six just reaffirms what is said in verse five, which should serve as a wake-up call to every lost person on earth. One of the great truths taught in the Bible, is that what ever condition the person is in, spiritually, when

139

they die, they will be in that condition when they stand before God.

Rev. 22:11 tells us, "He that is unjust, let him be unjust still: and he which is filthy, let him be filthy still: and he that is righteous, let him be righteous still: and he that is holy, let him be holy still."

I Tim. 5:24 says, "Some men's sins are open beforehand, going before to judgement; and some men they follow after."

This warning is to the Christian, and means that if we openly confess our sins here in this life, they go before the Lord and are forgiven.
I John 1:7,9.

If we do not confess them here in this life, they will be manifest at the Judgement Seat of Christ. *Rom. 14:10-12 and I Cor. 3:11-15.*

Verse four says, "...a living dog is better than a dead lion," for death ends all, here on earth. Since there is only one life to live, this side of eternity, we are encouraged to get the most out of that one life. I believe that God, who gives life, expects us to enjoy life under the sun. Jesus himself verifies this in *John 10:10b* when he said, "I am come that they might have life, and that they might have it more abundantly."

V-7.   *"Go thy way,"*

In going our way upon earth, we are not to ignore God in the going. On the contrary, we are told in Prov. 3:5-6, "Trust in the Lord with all thine heart; and lean not unto thine own understanding." V-6, "In ALL thy ways acknowledge him, and he shall direct thy paths."
"... eat thy bread with joy,"

We are told this in previous chapters; *Eccl. 2:24; 3:13; and 5:18*. Bread in the Bible, represents just about everything necessary to serve God. Jesus called himself the BREAD OF LIFE in *John 6:35,48.* We know that bread is a staple of our diet, and who would want to live without it? So, bread represents life, and we are to enjoy it to the fullest.

"*... and drink thy wine with a merry heart;*"

This is by no means a license for loose, licentious living. *Gal. 5:13* says, "For, brethren, ye have been called unto liberty; only use not liberty for an occasion to the flesh, but by love serve one another." *I Cor. 8:9* warns us, "But take heed lest by any means this liberty of yours become a stumbling block to them that are weak." Wine was usually used during feasts and to celebrate or honor royalty. *Gen. 14:18; I Sam. 16:20 and Eccl. 10:19.*

Bear in mind that the moderate use of wine is not forbidden in the Bible, regardless of what a lot of fundamentalists preach. It is called a "mocker" in *Prov. 20:1* and anyone deceived thereby is not wise. It is not for kings, according to *Prov. 31:4*, BUT verses 6 and 7 recommend it for a couple of reasons. In *I Tim. 3:3* one of the qualifications of a pastor or bishop is that he is not to be given to wine. However, in *I Tim. 5:23* Paul plainly says, "Drink no longer water, but use a little wine for thy stomachs sake and thine often infirmities."

"*... for God now accepteth thy works.*"

If man enjoys life within the bounds of God's instructions, then God accepts his work. But a sad and gloomy countenance does not glorify God. *Acts 2:46* says the new Christians did eat their meat with gladness and singleness of heart.

V-8.　　"*Let thy garments be always white:*"

Josephus, in his Antiquities (life and culture of early times) of the Jews, book VIII, 7:3 says of Solomon, that he was arrayed in white. This is probably the reason Jesus compared his clothes to the lilies of the field, in *Matt. 6:29*, "And yet I say unto you, that even Solomon in all his glory, was not arrayed like one of these." (lilies). The white garments represent purity and righteousness. We find Jesus commending a few of the saints in Sardis in *Rev. 3:4,5, and 18.*

Rev. 19:8 tells us that every one at the Marriage of the Lamb will be clothed in fine linen clean and white. *"... and let thy head lack no ointment."*

The anointing of the head represented the presence and power of God upon the person's life. The oil was typical of the Holy Spirit, and what Solomon is recommending here is that we always have the Holy Spirit with us, when we do anything for God.

In *Psa. 45:7* they were anointed with the oil of gladness. Jesus said in *Matt. 6:17*, "But thou, when thou fastest, anoint thy head, wash thy face." LOOK CLEAN AND HAPPY.

We have something to be happy about, for we have the Holy Spirit dwelling in us. *John 14:17; Rom. 8:11* and *I Cor. 3:16.*

Verses seven through twelve, encourages man to enjoy life and get the most out of it here on earth, or life under the sun. We have seen other Scriptures that say the same thing, *Ch. 2:24; 3:13 and 5:18.* What Solomon is saying here is, that for a man to get the most out of life, he needs to be happily married to a good woman and living in peace and harmony. *Pro. 18:22* says, "Who so findeth a wife findeth a good thing, and obtaineth favor with the Lord." On the other hand, *Prov. 21:9* says, "It is better to dwell in a corner of the house top, than with a brawling woman in a wide house." See *Prov. 19:13,14.*

V-9. *"Live joyfully with the wife whom thou lovest all the days of the life of thy vanity,"* Back in *Eccl. 7:26* the preacher sounds bitter when talking about women, but he is not talking about a happily married couple there. We remember that Solomon had more experience with women than any man that ever lived, for he had 700 wives and 300 concubines. With all of Solomon's experience with women, he came to the conclusion that one good wife was all any man needed to be happy, here in this life.

The apostle Paul gives the order of a scriptural home in *I Cor. 11:3-12. Prov. 5:18* says, "Let thy fountain be blessed: and rejoice with the wife of thy youth."

"... which he hath given thee under the sun, all the days of thy vanity:"

The word "vanity" is found 37 times in Ecclesiastes. The phrase "under the sun" is found 29 times. Solomon discovered that man at his best is still a VAIN character. BUT if he will follow God's blue print, he may still live a joyful life.

In order to get the very best mileage out of this life, we must say with David, in *Psa. 90:12*, "So teach us to number our days, that we may apply our hearts unto wisdom." Then David prayed in *Psa. 39:4*, "Lord, make me to know mine end, and the measure of my days, what it is; that I may know how frail I am."

God allots every man a certain number of days on earth, and leaves it up to man to make the most of his time. *Job 14:5; Job 7:1; Psa. 37:18. "for that is thy portion in this life,"*

"Only one life twill soon be past, only what's done for Christ will last." The word "portion" here, means our lot, our privilege, our fortune. It is our good fortune to do an honest days work, for an honest days pay, serve God to the best of our ability, and leave the rest to our maker.

V-10. *"Whatsoever thy hand findeth to do, do it with thy might;"*

I was brought up with the concept that if anything was worth doing it was worth doing right. Bear in mind that everything we do as Christians we are representing Jesus Christ. Thus Paul said in *Col. 2:23*, "And whatsoever ye do, do it heartily as to the Lord, and not unto men." See *Eph. 6:6-8*.

"... for there is no work, nor device, nor knowledge, nor wisdom, in the grave, whither thou goest."

The truth is that death severs every connection of man here on earth, and there is an urgency here in this statement to do our best. Jesus said in *John 9:4*, "I must work the works of him that sent me, while it is day: the night cometh, when no man can work." The ONLY thing that follows man at death is his works. *Eccl. 9:1; Rev. 14:13.*

Heb. 6:10, "For God is not unrighteous to forget your work and labour of love, which ye have shewed toward his name, in that ye have ministered to the saints, and do minister."

Finally, in *Amos 8:7*, "The Lord hath sworn by the excellency of Jacob, surely I will never forget any of their works."

In verse eleven, the first two words provoked my curiosity, as to their meaning. As I began to search the Scriptures and commentaries, I found no information, not even a hint at the meaning of "*I returned.*" However, since I believe that every word of the Bible is important, I will try to define the meaning of those two words.

V-11. "*I returned,*" Now my question is, where did he return from, and where did he return to? If we pay close attention to the wording of verses 7-10, Solomon has been speaking from man's view, and here in verse 11 he is turning from man's side of the discussion of life here on earth, or under the sun. He is taking God's side of the argument and giving God's perspective of the life of man, which happens to be opposite of man's idea of life. "*I returned, and saw under the sun,*"

What he sees in the next two verses, is how God looks at man and life under the sun. "that the race is not to the swift,"

The race here is not a foot race, automobile race, or horse race. In those races, the swift do win, and only one gets the prize. The preacher is referring to the RACE OF

144

LIFE, where all who run, wins. Paul talks about this race for life in *I Cor. 9:24,* "Know ye not that they which run in a race run all, but one receiveth the prize? (this is man's system of judging a race) So run that ye may obtain." Meaning that if you are in the race for eternal life, you are a winner whether you are the front runner of not. *Heb. 12:1* tells us how the race of life is run.

"... nor the battle to the strong,"

Heroes do not win wars, though they may do great feats of bravery. It takes every soldier to get the job done. Our God takes note of the UNSUNG heroes in the back field and those behind the front lines. David looked neither swift or strong, standing out there in front of Goliath, with that sling-shot in his hand. *I Sam. 17.* What Goliath didn't know was, that David had the God of heaven on his side; and God and one is a majority against any giant.

"... neither yet bread to the wise,"

Wisdom does not always make provision for the flesh. David knew hunger while fleeing from Saul. Peter experienced the pains of hunger. *Acts 10:10.* Our Lord himself knew what it meant to be hungry. *Matt. 4:2; and 21:18.* True wisdom feasts on the BREAD OF LIFE, which John speaks of in *John 6:35,48.* The lad with five loaves and two fishes in *John 6:9* didn't look wise at all, until he gave them to Jesus who fed 5,000. Even the disciples didn't think much about the idea until after their bellys were full of bread and fish.

"... nor yet riches to men of understanding,"

It is a sad fact, that many who possess great wealth make selfish use of it. *Psa. 37:16* says, "A little that a righteous man hath is better than the riches of many wicked." See *Prov. 11:28* and *13:7,8.*

"... nor yet favour to men of skill;"

Here again, many who are intelligent and skilled in certain endeavors, use their skills for the wrong purposes. In fact, Solomon who penned these very words, is a prime

145

example of one who had great skills, but lost favour with God through mis-use of them. *I Kings 11:1-11.*

I Kings 11:9 tells us, "And the Lord was angry with Solomon, because his heart was turned from the Lord God of Israel, which had appeared unto him twice."

"... but time and chance (opportunity) happeneth to them all."

Psa. 75:6,7 says, "For promotion cometh neither from the east, nor from the west, nor from the south." V-7, "But God is the judge (of who gets promoted): he putteth down one, and setteth up another." *Rom. 9:18*, "therefore hath he mercy on whom he will have mercy, and whom he will he hardeneth." In these and other verses we are made to understand God's sovereignty. *Isa. 14:24,26,27.*

The necessity of making the most of life "under the sun" is further seen in verse twelve. The last part of verse 11 says, Time and chance (opportunity) happeneth to them all." IF we take advantage of every opportunity to serve the Lord, our life here on earth will be greatly enhanced. Since we do not know how long or short our life will be, we must take every opportunity, and make the most of it.

V-12.   *"For man also knoweth not his time:"*

There is a warning to the evil ways of the wicked in *Prov. 6:14-15.* Solomon said, "Frowardness is in his heart, he deviseth mischief continually; he soweth discord." V-15, "Therefore shall his calamity come suddenly; suddenly he be broken without remedy." The believer is also warned to be watchful as to the Lord's return in *Mark 13:34- 37; I Thess. 5:1-3.*

When Solomon said, "For man also knoweth not his time", I believe we could also apply this to calamity and misfortune that might come our way, as christians. Our conduct in these times depends on the amount of the Amazing Grace of God we have acquired. *Prov. 27:1* tells us, "Boast not thyself of tomorrow; for thou knowest not what a day may bring forth." Here is another example of unexpected circumstances over which we have no control.

"*... as the fishes that are taken in an evil net,*"

God told Ezekiel that he would spread a net over the enemies of his people as a snare to stop them. He said in *Ezek. 12:13*, "My net also will I spread upon him, and he shall be taken in my snare." Again in *32:3*, "Thus saith the Lord God; I will therefore spread out my net with a company of many people; and they shall bring thee up in my net."

II Pet. 2:1-3 warns against "false teachers" who would with feigned words (false meaning) make merchandise of you." The Apostle Peter and Paul lists some of the pitfalls the christian encounters along the way. *I Tim. 4:1* says, "Now the Spirit speaketh expressly, that in the latter times some shall depart from the faith, giving heed to seducing spirits, and doctrine of devils." V-2, "Speaking lies in hypocrisy; having their conscience seared with a hot iron." As far back as *Josh. 23:13* God warned his people that there would be snares and traps for them,in this life, and that he, God, would not remove them. Here is another example:

"*... and as the birds that are caught in a snare;*"

Here again, God teaches man by a familiar subject, just how suddenly calamity may strike. It can come as sudden as *Prov. 7:23*, "Till a dart strike through his liver; as a bird hasteth to the snare, and knoweth not that it is for his life."

"*... so are the sons of men snared in an evil time when it falleth suddenly upon them.*"

I firmly believe the evil times are upon us, and the fowler has many snares set for the believer. Thank God for *Psa. 91:3* which tells us, "Surely he (God) shall deliver thee from the snare of the fowler, and from the noisome pestilence."

In *Eph. 5:16* Paul affirms that evil days were upon the earth during his time. He said in *V-15*, "See that ye walk circumspectly, not as fools, but as wise." *V-16*, "Redeeming the time, because the days are evil." In *Eph. 6:10-17* the apostle identifies our enemy and tells us how to stand up to him. *Jer. 6:15* and *8:12* describes a time of evil, when man will sin and not even be ashamed of it. BUT the sad part of these scriptures is, they are referring to God's people, Israel. I ask the question, are we not living in the same period of rebellion?

V-13.   *"This wisdom have I seen also under the sun, and it seemed great unto me:"*

I believe "this wisdom" means the wisdom of seeing life under the sun, as God sees it, which is the opposite of how man looks at life here earth. However, I think we could also say that "this wisdom" could be applied to the next 5 verses. When Solomon said, "It seemed great unto me" I don't think he was speaking of his own wisdom, but of God's. See *Eccl. 7:11-12.*

V-14.   This verse has been called both parable and allegory. Because the difference between the two is very slight, it could be either. A PARABLE is a short fictitious story that illustrates, or parallels, a moral attitude or religious principle. An ALLEGORY means to speak figuratively, or expression by means of symbolic language. In other words, an allegory is an emblem. With these examples in mind, let's look at the next few verses.

"There was a little city,"

Obviously this city is not named, therefore it is figurative. What is it a figure, type, or symbol of? In a sense, the church could be compared to the little city; for it had a small beginning. The church started with Jesus and his twelve apostles. *Matt. 16:18.*

"... and few men within it;"

Still symbolic of the beginning of the church, for next, after the assembling of the twelve, we find

Jesus appointing 70 more disciples in *Luke 10:1,17.*
BUT still few compared to worldly standards. Just
before Pentecost, we find the number has increased
to 120, in *Acts 1:15.*

It was not until the day of Pentecost and after, that
the church began to grow rapidly. See *Acts 2:41* and *4:4.*
"... and there came a great king against it,"

This king was evil, and represents the devil, which
has fought against the church since its inception. But we
have the promise of our Lord himself, in *Matt. 16:18*
that Satan and the gates of hell will not prevail or
destroy the church of the living God.

The true biblical churches today have more enemies
than any other time in its history; but even in Paul's day
he said in *I Cor. 16:9,* "For a great door and effectual is
opened unto me, and there are many adversaries." *Phil.
3:18* tells us, "For many walk, of whom I have told you
often, and now tell you even weeping, that they are the
enemies of the cross of Christ." BUT V-19 says, "Whose
end is destruction, whose god is their belly, and whose
glory is their shame, who mind earthly things."
"... and besieged it,"

To be besieged is to be surrounded on all sides by
armed forces. The word besiege also means, to worry or
cause distress, and Satan is good with these tactics.
Every cult that springs up is another tool of Satan, to
counteract the true church. Peter gives a good example
in *II Pet. 2:1-3.*
"... and built great bulwarks against it."

A bulwark is a solid wall-like structure built for
defense. We know Satan has gone to great lengths to
play havoc with the churches. Even though he knows
he cannot ultimately win, he can do great harm to the
local congregation.

His latest tool is to print the "Politically Correct
Bible," in which the Father and Son become "the parent

and the child." There will be no mention of the "Right hand of God" as this is offensive to left-handed people. "Our Father which art in heaven, Hallowed be thy name" will read: Father/Mother hallowed be your name, may your domain come.

As I said in our last lesson, I believe the PARABLE or ALLEGORY (since it could be either), is a beautiful symbol of the church of Jesus Christ and its head. We understand the little city to represent the humble beginning of the church, with her enemies besieging her. Now lets look within this little city.

V-15.   *"Now there was in it a poor wise man,"*

This also holds true for the Lord and his church, for our Lord was BOTH *poor* and *wise*. We read in *II Cor. 8:9*, "For we know the grace of our Lord Jesus Christ, that, though he was rich, (before he took the form of fleshly man)yet for your sakes he became poor, that ye through his poverty might be rich." *Matt. 8:20 and Luke 9:58* tell us that the foxes and birds fared better than Jesus did.

Christ was not only poor himself, but had a special affinity for the poor, of his time and for all time. *Matt. 5:3*, "Blessed are the poor in spirit." Then in *Matt. 11:5b*, "... the poor have the gospel preached to them." *Luke 6:20*, "And he lifted up his eyes on his disciples, and said, Blessed be ye poor: for yours is the kingdom of God." Special reward for the poor. Finally, concerning the poor, *James 2:5* says, "Hearken, my beloved brethren, Hath not God chosen the poor of this world rich in faith, and heirs of the kingdom which he hath promised to them that love him?"

Then, concerning our Lord's wisdom, we find in *Matt. 12:42*, "The Queen of the South (Sheba) came from the uttermost parts of the earth to hear the wisdom of Solomon; and BEHOLD A GREATER THAN SOLOMON IS HERE."

Mark 6:2 says, "And when the sabbath day was come, he began to teach in the synagogue: and many hearing him were astonished, saying, From whence hath this man these things? and what WISDOM is this that is given unto him, that such mighty works are wrought by his hands?" *Col. 2:3* tells us that in the Father and the Son are hid all the treasures of wisdom and knowledge.

Luke 2:40, "And the child grew, and waxed strong in spirit, FILLED WITH WISDOM: and the grace of God was upon him." *V-52*, "And Jesus increased in WISDOM and stature, and in favour with God and man." "*... and he by his wisdom delivered the city;*" Still the type and picture of Christ and his body, the church. One day this "poor man" will deliver the church from the earth. We are told in *Eph. 5:27*, "That he might present to himself a glorious church not having spot, or wrinkle, or any such thing; but that it should be holy and without blemish."

Then we have the marriage of the Lamb in *Rev. 19:7-9*. In this poor man's power to deliver, we are told in *I Thess. 1:10*, "And to wait for his Son from heaven, whom he raised from the dead, even Jesus which DELIVERED US FROM THE WRATH TO COME."
"*... yet no man remembered that same poor man.*"

This is the sin of ingratitude; like the nine lepers that were cleansed in *Luke 17:17-18*; but were not grateful enough to even thank their benefactor. We know the unsung heroes of christianity will one day be remembered. Jesus said in *Matt. 19:30*, "But many that are first shall be last; and the last shall be first." In *20:16*, "So the last shall be first, and the first last: for many be called but FEW ARE CHOSEN."

We are warned about forgetfulness in *Psa. 50:22*, "Now consider this, YE THAT FORGET GOD, lest I tear you in pieces, and there be none to deliver."

151

Finally, about forgetfulness; *Jer. 2:32* is a sad commentary: "Can a maid forget her ornaments, or a bride her attire? YET MY PEOPLE HAVE FORGOTTEN ME DAYS WITHOUT NUMBER."

Continuing the thought, that the "little city" and the "poor wise man" is a type of the church, and her head the Lord Jesus Christ; I believe the type will hold true for the rest of this chapter.

V-16.   *"Then said I, (this is Solomon referring to his own thinking) Wisdom is better than strength:"*

He said, back in *Ch. 7:19*, "Wisdom strengtheneth the wise more than ten mighty men which are in the city." The idea that wisdom is better than strength, was something Solomon discovered after he compared his wisdom with God's wisdom. Read *Eccl. 2:9,26.*

Prov. 2:9-10 lists some of the advantages of wisdom, "Then shalt thou understand righteousness and judgement, and equity; Yea, every good path. When wisdom entereth into thine heart, and knowledge is pleasant unto thy soul." *Prov. 4:5-8*, "Get wisdom, get understanding: forget it not; neither decline from the words of my mouth." *V-6*, "Forsake her not (wisdom) and she shall preserve thee." *V-7*, "Wisdom is the principle thing; therefore get wisdom: and with all thy getting get understanding." *V-8*, "Exalt her, and she shall PROMOTE thee: she shall bring thee honour, when thou dost embrace her."

"... nevertheless the poor man's wisdom is despised, and his words are not heard."

When Jesus returned to Nazareth in *Mark 6:3*, and began to teach, the people who heard him said, "Is not this the carpenter, the son of Mary, the brother of James, and Joses, and of Juda, and Simon? And are not his sisters here with us? And were offended at him."

152

Isa. 53:3 tells us our Lord would be "Despised and rejected of men; a man of sorrows, and acquainted with grief. And we hid as it were our faces from him, he was despised and we esteemed him not."

I believe we could say, without contradiction, that the greatest institution on earth, is the church that Jesus Christ established while he was here in person. YET, in the so-called churches today who gets most of the glory? We truly are living in the Laodicean church age of *Rev. 3:14-19.* Our Lord said to this church, that they said to the world, "I am rich, and increased with goods, and have need of nothing; and knowest not that thou art wretched, and miserable, and poor, and blind, and naked."

I am convinced that if Christ were on earth today, he would still be despised, and rejected, by the vast majority of mankind, including men of the professing christians. He would still tell them, "Ye do err, not knowing the truth, nor the power of God."

It would be no different than it was in John's day, when Jesus said in *John 15:18,24,* "If the world hate you, ye know it hated me before it hated you." *V-24,* "If I had not done among them the works which none other man did, they had not had sin: but now have they both seen and hated both me and my Father."

V-17.   *"The words of wise men are heard in quiet more than the cry (shouting) of him that ruleth among fools."*

True wisdom does not have to shout to be heard and received. There is a certain tranquility about the quiet words of wise men, that calm the hearer. I am reminded of Elijah, in *I Kings 19:12.* It was after the wind, the earthquake, and the fire that Elijah heard the STILL SMALL VOICE OF THE SPIRIT OF GOD, which gave him his directions. God told his people, in *Isa. 30:15,* that, "In returning and rest ye shall be saved; in quietness and in confidence shall be your

153

strength: and ye would not." Again, in *Isa. 42:2*, Isaiah said that Jesus would come and quietly dispense God's plan for man, and in *Matt. 12:18-21*, our Lord repeats the prophesy of Isaiah.

Concerning the phrase, "him that ruleth among fools," we read in *Eccl. 5:3b*, "...a fools voice is known by multitudes of words." *Eccl. 10:14a*, "....a fool also is full of words." He that ruleth among fools, is an example of the blind leading the blind.

V-18.   *"Wisdom is better than weapons of war:"*

Solomon said in verse 16, "Wisdom is better than strength." Here, it is better than weapons. This is true, because wisdom comes from God, according to *James 1:5; I Kings 4:29 and 5:12. Prov. 16:16* says, "How much better is it to get wisdom than gold! and to get understanding rather to be chosen than silver." *Eccl. 7:12* tells us, "Wisdom is a defense."

On the other hand, weapons are the product of man, and are instruments of destruction. However Paul tells us in *II Cor. 10:4,* "For the weapons of our warfare are not carnal, but mighty through God to the pulling down of strongholds." *V-5,* "Casting down imaginations and every high thing exalteth itself against the knowledge of God, and bringing into captivity every thought to the obedience of Christ."

"... but one sinner destroyeth much good."

This is true in the church. One old back-slidden church member, with a loose tongue, can turn the heads of people in the church family. Especially if those who listen to them, happen to be looking for an excuse to find fault. But *Prov. 10:18* says, "He that hideth hatred with lying lips, and he that uttereth a slander is a fool." Another way that the sinners in the church, destroy much good is by TALE-BEARING. God warned the people of Israel in *Lev. 19:16*, "Thou shalt NOT go up and down as a talebearer among the people." See *Prov. 11 13; Prov. 20:19; Prov. 26:20,22.*

154

We have a perfect illustration of one sinner destroying much good, in our first parents, Adam and Eve. When they fell, it affected the entire human race. *Rom. 5:12.*

Prov. 11:19, "An hypocrite with his mouth destroyeth his neighbor: but through knowledge shall the just be delivered." Could this be one reason that heaven rejoices when sinners get saved?

Luke 15:7 states, "I say unto you, that likewise joy shall be in heaven over one sinner that repenteth, more than over ninety and nine just persons, which need no repentance." *V-10*, "Likewise, I say unto you, there is joy in the presence of the angels of God over one sinner that repenteth."

Chapter 10

There are many verses in Ecclesiastes, dedicated to the subject of wisdom. One of the themes of the book is "Life under the sun," and Solomon reasons with man about this earthly life, both UNDER GOD, and apart from God. Solomon has contrasted folly and wisdom (Ch. 7). He has given the moderation of wisdom (Ch. 7), the strength of wisdom (Ch. 7), and the value of wisdom (Ch. 9). Here in chapter 10 he will give us some of the characteristics of wisdom.

V-1.   *"Dead flies cause the ointment of the apothecary to send forth a stinking savour (odor):"*

The word "apothecary" is a word from which we get the word pharmacy, and means, the place where the drugs and compounds are mixed for medicinal purposes. With this understanding, we can readily see the importance of keeping dead flies out of the ointment. But according to O.T. Scriptures, the apothecary was the place where healing ointment and sweet smelling perfumes were mixed. Read *Exod. 30:25,30* and *Exod. 37:29*. Here again, dead flies would most certainly not be appreciated. But the primary subject here in verse 1, is not about mixing perfumes and medicine, but the contrasting of folly and wisdom.

"... so doth a little folly him that is in reputation for wisdom and honor."

This phrase is a continuation of the last phrase of *9:18*, where the writer said, "One sinner destroyeth much good." A "little folly" from a wise person, is like the "little leaven" in *I Cor. 5:6*, where Paul said, "Your glorying is not good. Know ye not a little leaven leaveneth the whole lump?

157

Back in *Eccl. 2:13* Solomon said, "Then I saw that wisdom excelleth folly, as far as light excelleth darkness." The word "folly" means evil, wickedness, lewd behavior. This conduct does not become a person who is known for his or her wisdom and prudence. *Prov. 14:8* says, "The wisdom of the prudent is to understand his way: but the folly of fools is deceit."

Paul, in referring to Jesus, said in *Eph. 1:8*, "Wherein he hath abounded toward us in all wisdom and prudence." The application to the christian, is that our so-called SECRET sins and faults, not kept in check, will eventually poison the whole character. When we harbor certain sins, and make allowance for them in our lives, it causes us to fall IN grace, and OUT of favour and fellowship with God. Read II Chron. 7:14; Heb. 12:3-15. I believe we could also say that these dead flies represent, and are typical of, evil thoughts and unconfessed sin in our lives.

V-2. *"A wise man's heart is at his right hand; but a fool's heart at his left."*

This does not mean that between two people their heart could possibly be on opposite sides of their bodies; for we know that the organ that pumps the blood through our bodies, is on the same side of every human being. It seems to me that Solomon is comparing honour and inferiority, good and evil, right and wrong. In the Scriptures, Jesus is said to be sitting on the right hand of God. A place of honor. *Mark 16:19; Heb. 1:3; Heb. 8:1; 10:12; 12:2 and I Pet. 3:22.* The heart of a wise man is right with God, therefore he makes right choices, that honour God and blesses others. But the foolish person makes evil choices that lead himself and others astray.

Verse two refers to the right choices that a wise person makes, and the unwise choices that the foolish person makes. Verse three continues that thought.

V-3.   *"Yea also, when he that is a fool walketh by the way,"*

I believe the key word, in this phrase, is the little word "by". Mr. Webster tells us that one definition of this word is: "Being off the main route." Now we know that it has many other meanings, but I believe Solomon is saying that the foolish person can only walk incidental to, or off the main route of wisdom. We are told in *Prov. 10:14*, "Wise men lay up knowledge: but "the mouth of the foolish is near destruction." Then *Prov. 14:7* says, "Go from the presence of a foolish man, when thou perceivest not in him the lips of knowledge." *V-9* says, "Fools make a mock at sin: but among the righteous there is favour."

"... his wisdom faileth him, and he saith to everyone that he is a fool."

He reveals his character by his actions. *Prov. 15:2*, "The tongue of the wise useth knowledge aright: but the mouth of fools poureth out foolishness." In *V-14b*, "The mouth of fools feedeth on foolishness." See *Isa. 44:24-25*. Finally *Prov. 1:32* says, "For the turning away of the simple shall slay them, and the prosperity of fools shall destroy them." There is, possibly, another meaning to the phrase, "he saith to everyone that he is a fool." That in his ignorance and conceit, he thinks everyone he meets is a fool, and he is the only one who is right. Like the man in *Prov. 26:16*, which tells us, "The sluggard is wiser in his own conceit than seven men that can render a reason."

V-4.   *"If the spirit of the ruler rise up against thee,"*

It is a sad but true that many times foolish people are elevated to places of authority, who know nothing about dealing with people and their problems. We have an example of wicked rulers in *Psa. 2:2*, "The kings of the earth set themselves, and the rulers take counsel together, against the Lord, and against his anointed saying," V-3,"Let us break their bands asunder, and cast away their cords from us." If the spirit of the rulers rise up against us, it is because, "We wrestle not against

159

flesh and blood, but against principalities, against powers, against the *rulers of the darkness of this world*, against spiritual wickedness in high places." *Eph. 6:12.*
"... *leave not thy place,*"

In other words, don't tuck your tail between your legs and run from the devil. *Eph. 4:27* puts it this way, "Neither give place to the devil." Then in *Eph. 6:13,14*, "Having done all to stand, STAND THEREFORE." There is no place to quit.

In setting up the tabernacle in *Num. 2:17*, it was, "Every man in his place by their standards." However, in our society today, very few men find their place in the church, and even fewer set any kind of standard for their home or their church. Our God has done his part in setting the standards for home and church, but leaves it to his people to uphold them. *Isa. 49:22 and 62:10.*

Psa. 89:28 and 111:8 declares that God's promises and commandments stand fast forever. It is because of His faithfulness that we are encouraged to be faithful in our service for Him. *I Cor. 16:13; Gal. 5:1; Phil. 1:27; 4:1; I Thess. 3:8 and II Thess. 2:15.*
"... *for yielding pacifieth great offenses.*"

I believe there are two ways to look at this phrase, for we are told in *James 4:7*, "Submit yourselves therefore to God. Resist the devil and he will flee from you." Therefore to yield to Satan on doctrinal truths would be cowardice. On the other hand, if it is of a trivial nature, our Lord said it was better to agree with our adversary. See *Matt. 5-25 and Luke 12:58-59.*

It is in making these choices that we must exercise the wisdom of God that we make the right one.

In the study of the characteristics of wisdom, we find that one characteristic is the ability to make right choices (most of the time, at least, for wisdom does not make one perfect). This is seen in verse five.

V-5. *"There is an evil which I have seen under the sun, as an error which proceedeth from the ruler:"*

It seems to me, that Solomon is referring to the fact that when a ruler or person in a position of authority and respect, falls into disrepute, and causes people to loose respect for him, and for the office he holds, that many are hurt. Many times the wounds run deep, and are even life-threatening.

We are warned against this in *I Cor. 8:9-12*, where Paul warns against our overstepping the bounds of liberty. Someone has well said that "absolute power corrupts absolutely." Again we use the example in *Psa. 2:2* which says, "The kings of the earth set themselves, and the rulers take counsel together, against the Lord, and against his anointed, saying," *V-3*, "Let us break their bands asunder, and cast away their cords from us." In *Eph. 6:12* we are warned against the "rulers of the darkness of this world." When we put to much confidence in man and the flesh, we are headed for a fall. *Jer. 17:5*, "Thus saith the Lord; cursed be the man that trusteth in man, and maketh flesh his arm, and whose heart departeth from the Lord."

V-6. *"Folly is set in great dignity, and the rich sit in low place."*

Position does not build character, but does reveal and expose character for good or bad. Nor does wealth improve character.

Our character is not what others think of us, not even what we think of ourselves, but what we are inside, or the inner-man. This is what God sees when he looks at us. Character is often found in poor people, and folly and foolishness found in the wealthy and upper-class of society. We have an example in *I Sam. 2:7-9*. Here we find that God has a say in who is exalted and who is made low.

In speaking of folly, *Prov. 15:21* tells us, "Folly is joy to him that is destitute of wisdom: but a man of under-

161

standing walketh uprightly." Example: The ministry is supposed to be a position of dignity, but there is much folly and hypocrisy among ministers. God had much to say about this through Jeremiah. See *Jer. 23:9-14,21*.

Many misguided souls associate wealth and riches with dignity, but this is not necessarily so. Jesus speaks of the "deceitfulness of riches" in *Matt. 13:22*. We find a contrast of the rich and poor in *Prov. 13:7*, "There is that maketh himself poor, yet hath great riches."

V-7.   *"I have seen servants upon horses, and princes walking as servants upon the earth."*

This verse bears out the theory of *Prov. 13:7* as horses were, more or less, reserved for nobility. As Jeremiah says in *Jer. 17:25*, "kings and princes." On the other hand, if servants rode at all, they rode donkeys, but usually had to walk. BUT God in His Sovereignty and power can reverse the order, whether it be princes, kings, or nations, and do it at His will. We read in *Job 12:19,21*, "He leadeth princes away spoiled, and overthroweth the mighty." *V-21*, "He poureth contempt upon princes, and weakeneth the strength of the mighty." *Job 34:18-19*, "Is it fit (for man) to say to a king, thou art wicked? and to princes ye are ungodly? How much less to him that accepteth not the persons of princes, not regardeth the rich more than the poor? for they are all the work of his hands."

Solomon is discussing the characteristics of wisdom, here in the tenth chapter. Verse six tells us that folly and foolishness is sometimes found in high places, and among people in authority, It still takes its toll of the person and/or position. It seems to me that this is the meaning of verse eight.

V-8.   *"He that diggeth a pit shall fall into it:"*

This is a proverb, and in fact is repeated in *Prov. 26:27*. It expresses the need to exercise caution where folly is present. Folly is like the leaven which Paul

162

speaks of in *I Cor. 5:6* and *Gal. 5:9* where he said, "A little leaven leaveneth the whole lump."

Folly, iniquity, and sin is a trap, no matter where it is found, according to the Scriptures. *Psa. 7:15,16; Psa. 9:15 and 10:2.* The PIT is used to trap animals, and usually are so cleverly disguised that the one who digs it must be careful not to fall into his own trap.

"... *and whoso breaketh a hedge, a serpent shall bite him.*"

Here again, caution is to be exercised when removing a hedge, for snakes may be making their home there. The reference here seems to be the difficulty in removing folly from a person known for wisdom, or removing evil, once it is entrenched in an organization. I believe this is the reason for the parable of the tares in *Matt. 13:24-30.*

V-9.   "*Whoso removeth stones shall be hurt therewith;*"

The principle of using caution is continued here, in the handling of stones. Be careful that you don't drop one on your foot, and the larger the stone, the more caution must be taken in their handling.

The last phrase of verse 10 says, "Wisdom is profitable to direct." Wisdom will direct our ways, works, and our words, which verse 11 is referring to. Verse 11 gives the consequences of the action of those without wisdom.

V-11.   "*Surely the serpent will bite without enchantment;*"

We know that the serpent, in Scriptures, represents evil. *Gen. 3:1* tells us, "Now the serpent was more subtle than any beast of the field which the Lord God had made." Then in *Rev. 12:9* we read, "And the great dragon was cast out, *that old serpent,* called the Devil, and Satan, which deceiveth the whole world: he was cast out into the earth, and his angels were cast out with him... See also *Rev. 20:2.* There in *Gen. 3:13* Eve told the Lord, "The serpent BEGUILED me, and I did eat." Old slew foot is still in the BEGUILING business today. We also have the illustration of the fiery serpents, and the brazen serpent of *Num. 21:5-9.* The brazen serpent was to be a constant reminder to Israel, of their sin of murmuring against God and His man Moses. BUT the people gradually began to worship this brass serpent on this pole. In *II Kings 18:1-7* Hezekiah destroyed it.

The lesson here, seems to be, that sin will turn on the one who indulges in it, without warning, and it has destructive powers. The word "enchantment" here is an interesting word. Mr. Webster tells us the meaning of the word "enchant." It means to influence by charms and incantation. It also means to bewitch, to attract and move deeply, and to rouse to ecstatic admiration. But Solomon tells us that SIN has such power, that it can destroy WITHOUT these enchantments.

"... and he that cleaveth wood shall be endangered thereby."

The timber industry is another dangerous business, and has cost many lives through timber falling, hauling, and sawing. In *Deut. 19:5* we find the allegory of two men chopping wood, and the axe flying off the handle and killing one of them. REMEMBER the writer is referring to the danger and the difficulty of removing folly and iniquity from high places.

V-10   *"If the iron be blunt,"*

There are not very many things more provoking than a dull axe. You will do a lot of chopping, but there will not be many chips flying. Like the modernists of today, there is a lot of activity but very little that glorifies God.

"... and he do not whet the edge, then must he put to more strength:"

In other words, the duller the axe, the more labour it takes to make it cut, and the longer it takes to sharpen the cutting edge when you do file it.

"... but wisdom is profitable to direct."

Here we see the value of wisdom. It gives direction, whether digging the pit, cutting the hedge, handling

164

stones, cutting wood, or removing folly and evil from high places.

Prov. 8:11 says of wisdom, "For wisdom is better than rubies; and all things that may be desired are not to be compared to it."

"... and a babbler is no better."

In *Acts 17:18* Paul was called a "babbler" by the philosophers of Athens. A babbler is one who talks foolishly, one who PRATTLES, or talks excessively. This is what the philosophers of our day, still think of the Holy Word of God. They think like Festus, in *Acts 26:24* who told Paul, "Paul, thou art beside thy self; much learning doth make thee mad." V-25, "But he said, I am not mad, most noble Festus; but speak forth the words of truth and soberness."

Here again, wisdom would prevent this type of behavior in the christian. *Prov. 17:27*, "He that hath knowledge spareth his words: and a man of understanding is of excellent spirit." *Prov. 10:19,* "In the Multitude of words there wanteth not sin: but he that refraineth his lips is wise."

V-12. *"The words of a wise man's mouth are gracious;"*

Solomon said it another way in *Prov. 10:32*, "The lips of the righteous know what is acceptable; but the mouth of the wicked speaketh frowardness." It is said of Jesus in *Luke 4:22*, "And all bare him witness, and wondered at the *gracious words* which proceeded out of his mouth And they said, is not this Joseph's son?" The answer of course is NO, he was the step-son of Joseph, and the Son of God.

"... but the lips of a fool will swallow up himself."

Prov. 10:14, "Wise men lay up knowledge: but the mouth of the foolish is near destruction."

Concerning the word "fool", *Psa. 14:1* tells us, "The FOOL hath said *in his heart,* There is no God. They are corrupt, they have done abominable works, there is none that doeth good."

Prov. 12:15, "The way of a fool is right in his own eyes: BUT he that hearkeneth unto counsel is wise."

Prov. 15:5, "A fool despiseth his fathers instruction: but he that regardeth reproof is prudent."

Prov. 18:2, "A fool hath no delight in understanding, but that his heart may discover itself."

From verses 11-14, Solomon is comparing the words of a wise man, with the words of the foolish. He tells us in the last phrase of V-12 that "The lips of a fool will swallow him up." As the old saying goes, "He lets his mouth overload his grace."

V-13. *"The beginning of the words of his mouth is foolishness:"*

From the beginning to the end of his speech, the foolish person displays their nature. *Prov. 15:2* says, "The tongue of the wise useth knowledge aright: but the mouth of fools poureth out foolishness." *Prov. 17:7* tells us, "Excellent speech becometh not a fool. Much less do lying lips a prince."

"... and the end of his talk is mischievous madness."

The longer this person talks, the worse he gets, and ends with wickedness or insanity. The Apostle Paul warns against this very thing in *Rom. 16:17-18*. He said in *V-18b* that this type of person, "By good words and fair speeches deceives the hearts of the simple." This same Apostle tells the Corinthians that he was NOT a man of eloquent words. Read *I Cor. 2:1-5*.

V-14. *"A fool also is full of words:"*

He can talk longer and say less than anyone else. We are reminded of *Eccl. 5:2b*, "Therefore let thy words be few." Then *V-3b*, "A fools voice is known by multitude of words." This kind of person thinks they know everything, any subject you mention, they have an opinion about it. The three hardest words for this type person is: "I DON'T KNOW."

"... a man cannot tell what shall be "

I believe the preacher means, you cannot tell from a man who is full of words, which words are to be taken for truth and which are in error. This is possibly what *I John 4:1* is referring to, when he said, "Beloved, believe not every spirit, but try the spirits whether they are of God: because many false prophets are gone out into the world."

"... and what shall be after him, who can tell him?

It is hard to tell what direction a person like this is going, because they have baffled you with words. See *I Cor. 14:6-12.* When preaching or teaching the Word of God, we need to give a distinctive sound, make the message plain. It is also hard to tell this person's destination or spirituality. This is the reason every child of God needs the spirit of discernment.

I think there is another meaning here, and it is this. Who can tell what this type of persons influence will be on those who follow them?

V-15. *"The labour of the foolish wearieth every one of them,"*

The words and works of the foolish adversely affects those who know the truth, but who are destitute of discernment. Jesus said in *John 8:32,* "And ye shall know the truth, and the truth shall make you free."

"... because he knoweth not how to go to the city."

This person doesn't have sense enough to find his way to town. Though I had rather think, that the CITY referred to here, means the "City of refuge," found in the books of *Num. 35; Josh. 21 and I Chron. 6:57.* This was a place for a person who killed another person without malice, where they could be safe until the case was judged by those appointed to such office.

The foolish person does not have the wisdom to direct him to the city or place of refuge, which we know is Jesus Christ. *Psa. 46:1.* "God is our refuge and strength, a very present help in trouble." *Psa. 62:7-8- Heb. 6:18-19.*

167

So far, in this chapter, Solomon has been discussing the characteristics of wisdom of individuals, and the folly of those who are destitute of it. Now he is referring to the king, or person in authority over others.

V-16.   *"Woe to thee, O land,"*

This word "woe" is used to express grief, distress, or regret. It also means calamity, or affliction, and can be physical, economical, spiritual decay. The word "woe" is used throughout the Bible as a warning from God to man, and in the N.T. Jesus used this word often to warn different groups, "Woe unto thee Chorazin! woe unto thee Bethsaida! Matt. 11:21a; "Woe unto the world," *Matt 18:7*; "Woe unto ye blind guides, *Matt. 23:16;* Then in *Rev. 8:13* we find, "Woe, woe, woe to the inhabiters of the earth." In *Rev. 11:13-14* we find mention of the second and third woe. When we see this word, it means judgement is soon to be pronounced.

"... when thy king is a child,"

I believe this phrase refers to the ruler or person in authority being unskilled, or childish, in making decisions that affect others. We find the results of children ruling in *Isa. 3:4-5,11*. In *I Cor. 14:20* the Apostle Paul told the Corinthians, "Brethren, be not children in understanding: howbeit in MALICE be ye children, but in understanding be men." A child never holds hatred in his heart, but on the other hand, he never thinks things through to a logical conclusion. The Child is mostly moved by selfish desires, and whims, and is for the most part greedy. There are exceptions to the rule, and yours probably are.

The king may be adult in years, and a child in his ability to make mature decisions.

"... and thy princes eat in the morning!"

The word "eating" here refers to feasting and drinking all night, until early morning, or starting the day in such a manner. *Isa 5:11* warns against this. He said, "WOE unto them that rise up early in the morning, that they may follow strong drink; that continue until night, till wine inflame them." Here in *Isa. 5:8-21* you will find six woes pronounced upon Israel.

V-17.   "*Blessed art thou,*'(*the opposite of woe, and means good things from God*), *O land, when thy king is the son of nobles,*"

This person has character, and makes noble decisions that are a blessing to those who are under him. Jesus used Abraham as an example of this principle in *John 8:39,* "They answered and said unto him (Jesus), Abraham is our father. Jesus saith unto them, IF YE WERE ABRAHAM'S CHILDREN, YE WOULD DO THE WORKS OF ABRAHAM."

"*... and thy princes eat in due season, for strength, and not for drunkness!*"

They eat at the proper time, and for the proper reasons. In *Phil. 3:17-19* Paul warns against the crowd whose god is their belly.

V-18.   "*By much slothfulness the building decayeth;*"

The word "slothful" means laziness. We find a prime example of laziness in *Prov. 24:30-34.* BUT this phrase is not confined to a physical building only, but to an individual,or organization, including the local church. In every thing there must be a preventive maintenance program to replenish and refurbish. A chain is only as strong as its weakest link.

"*... and through idleness of the hands the house droppeth through.*"

If you don't repair the roof, it will fall in on your head. When you find a leak in your roof,and don't repair it it will get worse. Like a nagging woman, both are a drip. *Prov. 19:13.* Then *Prov. 27:15* tells us, "A continual dropping (drip) in a very rainy day and a contentious woman are alike." Both are an aggravation.

In *Amos 6:3-6* we find Israel in a state of disrepair, and debauchery. BUT in *Amos 9:11* God repairs the breaches.

Many churches have been destroyed for lack of watching and keeping alert for weak spots, such as gossip, and slander. Laziness also has no place in the work of God.

In our last lesson we discussed the subject of laziness. We just want to leave a brief thought with you, concerning that discussion. No doubt you have heard the old saying "An idle mind is the devil's playground." While this exact phrase is not found in the Bible, the concept is scriptural, for we read in *Prov. 19:15*, "Slothfulness casteth into deep sleep; and an idle soul shall suffer hunger." See *Ezek. 16:49*.

V-19.   *"A feast is made for laughter, and wine maketh merry:"*

The Jews held many feasts throughout the year, and most of them was attended with joy and laughter, and praise to God. However there were also solemn feasts of mourning. *Deut. 16:15; Psa. 81:3; Lam. 2:7.* In *Eccl. 3* the writer said there was a right and wrong time for everything under heaven. In *V-4* he tells us there is, "Time to weep, and a time to laugh; a time to mourn, and a time to dance." Then in *V-13* we read, "And also that every man should eat and drink, and enjoy the good of all his labour, it is the gift of God." BUT, if we abuse and mis-use these privileges we suffer the consequences. Lets think about that phrase, "And wine maketh merry." Contrary to what a lot of ignorant people think, the use of wine is not forbidden in the Bible, but we are warned about the abuse of it. In *Psa. 104:15* we read, "*Wine* that maketh glad the heart of man, and *oil* to make his face to shine, and *bread* which strengtheneth man's heart." In *Judges 9:13* there is a peculiar verse that says, "And the vine said unto them, should I leave my wine, which cheereth God and man, and go to be promoted over the trees?" On the other hand, *Prov. 20:1* tells us, "Wine is a mocker, strong drink is raging: and whosoever is deceived thereby is not wise." So here we have the wrong use of a product that God meant for good.

"... *but money answereth all things.*"

This is how the world looks at money, but we know that there are some things that money cannot buy. We are told in *I Tim. 6:10* that the, "Love of money is the ROOT of all evil: which while some coveted after, they have erred from the faith, and pierced themselves through with many arrows." Here again, it is the wrong concept of wealth that brings sorrow.

V-20. *"Curse not the king, no not in thy thought;"*

This refers back to *V-16*, where we are told that the king may be childish, and may seek revenge on those who says ugly things about him. In *Exod. 22:28* we are told to keep the king's commandment because of our relationship to God, but here in *V-20*, it seems to be for personal safety.

"... *and curse not the rich in thy bedchamber:*"

There is an old proverb that says, "Walls have ears." In *II Kings6:12* we are told that Elisha the prophet knew what the king had said in his bedchamber. Jesus warns us that, "There is nothing covered, that shall not be revealed; neither hid, that shall not be known." "Therefore whatsoever ye have spoken in darkness shall be heard in the light; and that which ye have spoken in the ear in closets shall be proclaimed upon the house tops." *Luke 12:2-3*

"... *for a bird of the air shall carry the voice and that which hath wings shall tell the matter.*"

The phrase, "A little bird told me," may have had its beginning from this verse. Though I rather think this phrase refers to the use of carrier pigeons, which has been used for thousands of years. We know that we must use discretion when we speak of rulers (even Clinton) lest we fall into the category of those in *Jude 8-10* and *II Pet. 2:10-11*.

Chapter 11

We read in the last part of *Rev. 14:13*, "And their works do follow them." I believe we could apply verse one to this principle. This verse is known as a "metaphor" or figure of speech, or simile.

V-1.   *"Cast thy bread upon the waters: for thou shalt find it after many days."*

The key to understanding this verse is the word "sharing," which we are encouraged to do throughout the Bible. In fact, Jesus teaches this concept; that giving enhances all other graces. *Matt. 19:21.* The word "cast" denotes effort, meaning we are to put our energy into sharing with others.

The word "bread" has a two-fold meaning. It not only means physical food, but also means we are to share the "Living Bread" of *Jn. 6:31-35.* Bread is the "staff of life" both physical and spiritual. *Jn. 6:51.* It seems to me that the meaning of casting our bread upon the waters, means giving without expecting a definite or specific return.

The word "waters" could also represent the masses of people around the world, which is the reason we support missions. It is a command. *Mark 16:15.* Let us take a closer look at the phrase, "For thou shalt find it after many days." We have a habit of expecting immediate results, when we ask God for some particular need. "Many days" can mean either time in, days, weeks, months, years, or even eternity. Some *of the* good deeds *we* do here, may be rewarded only when we get to heaven. But Jesus assures us in *Matt. 10:42* that we will be rewarded. Paul says in *Gal. 6:9*, "And let us not be weary in well doing: for in due season we shall reap, if we faint not."

Heb. 5:10, "For God is not unrighteous to forget your work and labour of love, which ye have shewed toward his name, in that ye have ministered to the saints, and do minister."

V-2.   *"Give a portion to seven and also to eight"*

We understand the number "seven" to be the number of completion, and it would seem that the number "eight" simply means, stretch even farther. In fact, Jesus teaches this truth in *Matt. 5:38-41.*

We have a picture of a generous person in *Psa. 112:9.* David said,"He hath dispersed, he hath given to the poor; his righteousness endureth forever; his horn shall be exalted with honor."

In *Luke 6:30* Jesus said, "Give to every man that asketh of thee; and of him that taketh away thy goods ask them not again."

I believe this statement also means, don't confine your charity to one source, but spread it around and claim the promise of *Prov. 11:25,* "The liberal soul shall be made fat: and he that watereth shall be watered also himself." This kind of liberality is what Paul is speaking of in *II Cor. 9:6-13* and *II Cor. 8:1-6.*

"... for thou knowest not what evil shall be upon the earth."

We never know when the opportunity to help others may be taken away and we will be in need of help. Paul confirms this in *Gal. 6:1,* where he said, "Brethren if a man be overtaken in a fault, ye which are spiritual, restore such an one in the spirit of meekness: *considering thyself, lest thou also be tempted."*

Also here in *Gal. 6:7-9* we have God's unfailing law of sowing and reaping. *Eph. 5:16* tells us to, "Redeem the time, because the days are evil." *V-17* says, "Be not unwise, but understanding what the will of the Lord is."

In the last phrase of verse two, we read "For thou knowest not what evil shall be upon the earth." The meaning seems to be, that there are forces at work, in the universe, over which we have no control. We know this to be true. Verse 3 continues this idea.

V-3.   *"If the clouds be full of rain, they empty themselves upon the earth:"*

This is one part of nature that man has absolutely no control over. The meteorologist can check the atmosphere and make predictions, but they have no control over the elements that produce our weather. Even though we have no control over the evil, and the forces of nature, we must be ready to deal with them. By God's grace we will overcome ALL forces that we face. Listen to *Prov. 22:3*, "A prudent man foreseeth the evil, (realizes it can happen) and hideth himself: (in the Lord) but the simple pass on and are PUNISHED."

Likewise there are times of testing and trials from the Lord, that we must be prepared to meet and overcome. Job had to learn this lesson. In *Job 23:10* he said, "But he knoweth the way I take: when he hath tried me, I shall come forth as gold." Then in *Job 34:36* God said, "My desire is that Job may be tried unto the end because of his answers for wicked men." This statement by God was because of *V-35*, "Job hath spoken without knowledge, and his words were without wisdom." In *James 1:12* we read, "Blessed is the man that endureth temptation: for when he is tried, he shall receive the crown of life, which the Lord hath promised to them that love him."

We know not when or to what degree the testing will be, but we do know that our Lord will never put more on us than we can bear. *I Cor 10:13*.

"... and if the tree fall toward the south, or toward the north, in the place where the tree falleth, there it shall be."

Here again, we have no control over when the tree falls, nor in what direction it falls. We accept the fact that it has fallen, so it is with the things in life, over

175

which we have no control. We face setbacks and disappointments with confidence in the God we serve, because of Scriptures such as *Rom. 8:36-37,* "Who shall separate us from the love of Christ? shall tribulation, or distress, or persecution, or famine, or nakedness, or peril, or sword?" *V-36,* "As it is written, For thy sake we are killed all the day long; we are accounted as sheep for the slaughter." *V-37,* "NAY, in all things we are more than conquerors through him that loved us."

Keeping our eyes fixed on Christ is the only answer for anything and everything that happens to us in this life.

V-4.   *"He that observeth the wind shall not sow, and he that regardeth the clouds shall not reap."*

The farmer must take the weather into consideration when he plants or gathers his crops, BUT if he is to cautious, he will never get the job done. He may even use the weather as an excuse not to do anything. So, a prudent man will use discretion in everything he does. The Christian must use the wisdom from God, when going against forces we have no control over. In fact, there is no guarantee that we will not fail. But if we do, we give God the glory anyway.

We have learned from the first four verses of the eleventh chapter that there are forces of nature at work in the universe, over which we have no control, and verse five is continuing that thought.

V-5.   *"As thou knowest not what is the way of the spirit,"*

There are some mysteries in this life that man will never unravel, and here in V-5 we find two of them. We find an example of the mystery of the Spirit in *John 3:8,* where Jesus is explaining the new birth to Nicodemus as he said, "The wind bloweth where it listeth, (where it wants to) and thou hearest the sound thereof, but canst not tell whence it cometh, (where it came from and where it started) and whither it goeth: (where and when it stops after it passed you) so is every one that is born of the spirit."

In my humble opinion, the new birth is easier experienced than explained. *"It's better felt than telt."* If Jesus could not explain it to Nicodemus' satisfaction, don't expect me to make you understand the new birth and the way of the Spirit. In *John 3:9* Nicodemus said, "How can these things be?"

There are many mysteries in the Bible that the unregenerate person will never know, according to the Apostle Paul, in *I Cor. 2:7-8;* Also in Matt. 13:11 and Luke 8:10. To the born-again believer, the Holy Spirit reveals these hidden truths. *I Cor. 2:14-16.* Then in *I Cor. 4:1* we are called "Stewards of the mysteries of God."
"... nor how the bones do grow in the womb of her that is with child:"

David said in *Psa. 139:14-15,* "I will praise thee, for I am fearfully and wonderfully made: marvelous are thy works (in the creation of the human body) and that my soul knoweth right well."

Meaning he was thoroughly convinced of the fact that man is the highest order of God's creation. Man has absolutely no control over how a baby is formed in the womb, nor what it will look like when it is born. Neither can man measure the capacity of the child to love or hate. BUT GOD knows everything there is to know about that unborn child. *Job 31:15; 34:19; Prov. 22:2* and *Isa. 44:2,24.*

There are many things that God will not trust man with the knowledge of, for the reason Paul gives in *I Cor. 2:8.* We understand this to be the meaning of in the next phrase.
"... even so thou knowest not the works of God who maketh all."

In the providence of a sovereign God, there are some things that the finite mind of man will NEVER know. We believe that God alone is omniscient, which means complete or perfect knowledge. *Matt. 24:36* tells us, "But of that day and hour (concerning the coming of the Lord) knoweth no man, no not the angels of heaven, but my Father only." See *Eccl. 8:17*

One reason man cannot know all the works of God is seen in *Psa. 145:17* where the Psalmist said, "The Lord is *righteous* in all his ways, and *holy* in all his works." UNREGENERATE MAN IS NEITHER.

Eccl. 7:13 says, "Consider the work of God: for who can make that straight, which he hath made crooked?"

According to *Eccl. 3:11* there are some things about creation that man will never know. Solomon said, "He hath made every thing beautiful in his time: also he hath set the world in their heart, so that no man can find out the work that God maketh from the beginning to the end."

We have learned from the preceding verses that there are forces at work in the universe that only the Sovereign God of creation has control over. There are many things like creation, life, survival of mankind that God just will not trust man with. We continue this thought in verse six.

V-6.   *"In the morning sow thy seed, and in the evening withhold not thine hand:"*

Here is another area over which man has no control. He may control the sowing and the reaping, but as to the production of the crop, that is in the hands of the one who controls the elements. I believe we could apply the sowing of seed here to all of life, of which there are many facets. For instance, in *Gen. 2:15* we read, "And the Lord God took the man, and put him into the garden of Eden to dress it and to keep it." (Maintain its beauty).

We do not depend on one facet of life to sustain us, therefore after we have sown, or planted the seed, there are other areas in which we must keep busy, so the writer says, "... and in the evening withhold not thy hand." Don't sit down and fold your hands and wait for the harvest. The Palmist said in *Psa. 104:23*, "Man goeth forth

178

unto his work and to his labour until the evening." *V-24,* "O Lord, how manifold are thy works! In wisdom thou hast made them all: the earth is full of thy riches." Then in *Luke 9:62* Jesus said, "No man having put his hand to the plough, and looking back, is fit for the kingdom of God." IN OTHER WORDS, KEEP ON PLOUGHING. *"... for thou knowest not whither shall prosper, either this or that, or whether they both shall be alike good."*

Regardless of what pursuit of life we are engaged in, success or failure is in the hands of God. James tells us in *James 4:15,* "For ye ought to say, If the Lord will, we shall live, and do this, or that." For the child of God, we have the promise of our Lord in *Matt. 6:33,* "But seek ye first the kingdom of God, and his righteousness; and all these things shall be added unto you."

If I understand *Eccl. 8:15* and *9:7-10,* God wants his children to enjoy life, and they will when they put Him first in every endeavor. There is much said about seed and planting, in the Word of God. Therefore I believe we may rightly apply this verse to the spiritual seed that the christian is supposed to sow. We do the planting or sowing of the seed, which is the Word of God according to *Luke 8:11,* where Jesus said, "Now the parable is this: The seed is the word of God." It is by the Spirit of the Word that we are born into the family of God. Read *John 3:5* where our Lord said, "Verily, verily, I say unto thee, Except a man be born of water and of the Spirit he cannot enter the kingdom of God." Then in *I Pet. 1:23* we are told, "Being born again not of corruptible seed, but of uncorruptible BY THE WORD OF GOD, which liveth and abideth forever."

We are to plant the seed, or water the seed, but leave the increase to God. Paul gives the order in *I Cor. 3:3-7.* As Solomon said, "For thou knowest whither shall prosper" (the planting or the watering).

179

BUT we are promised a harvest in the future in *Psa. 126:6*, "He that goeth forth and weepeth, bearing precious seed, shall doubtless come again with rejoicing, bringing his sheaves with him." (increase).

We understand from verse six that we are to continue our labour for Christ and leave the increase to God. As Paul teaches the Corinthians in *I Cor. 3: 6-7*, "I have planted, Apollos watered; but God gave the increase." *V-7*, "So then neither is he that planteth anything, neither he that watereth; But God that giveth the increase."

V-7. *"Truly the light is sweet, and a pleasant thing it is for the eyes to behold the sun:"*

I believe the word "light" here is referring to the light of life, or the morning of youth and vigor. When we read the next several verses, we understand the writer to challenge the young people to enjoy life, BUT to enjoy it through their service to God. It is a pleasant thing to behold the sun, especially in our youth, but how much greater value for all eternity, to behold the Son of righteousness. See *Eccl. 12:1*.

The Psalmist said in *Psa. 56:13*, "For thou hast delivered my soul from death: wilt not thou deliver my feet from falling, that I may walk before God in the light of the living."

Life under the *s u n* is one thing, and should be enjoyed: but the long range benefits are only to be found in living life in the *S O N*. In *Job 33:30*, he praised God for the ability to "Bring back his soul from the pit, to be enlightened with the light of the living." ONLY the person living for Christ is truly enlightened.

David said in *Psa. 27:1*, "The Lord is my light and my salvation; whom shall I fear? the Lord is the strength of my life; of whom shall I be afraid?"

V-8. *"But if a man live many years, and rejoice in them all;"*

Solomon tells us in several places in this book that there is nothing wrong with enjoying life, here under the sun. *Chs. 2:24; 3:12-13,22; and 5:18.* The problem lies in living for this life to the exclusion of God. Even if we rejoiced in every year of life here on earth,it would not compare to the DARKNESS of all eternity. Thus we have the warning of the next phrase.

"... yet let him remember the days of darkness; for they shall be many;"

While man is enjoying life here on earth, he is to be ever mindful of the darkness of those without Christ. It is said of John the Baptist in *Luke 1:79* that he came, "To give light to them that sit in darkness and in the shadow of death, to guide our feet into the way of peace."

Prov. 2:13 speaks of those "Who leave the paths of uprightness, to walk in the ways of darkness."

Prov. 4:19, "The way of the wicked is as darkness: they know not at what they stumble."

Isa. 60:2 speaks of a time when darkness shall be upon the earth, in fact, he said, "For, behold, the darkness shall cover the earth, and GROSS DARKNESS THE PEOPLE: but the Lord shall arise upon thee and his glory shall be seen upon thee." (Israel)

This book we call the Bible, not only teaches us how to live well, but how to die well. To me, this is what the few remaining verses teaches. The ceaseless ages of eternity should challenge us to prepare for life after death.

"All that cometh is vanity."

Psa. 39:5 tells us, "Behold, thou hast made my days as an handbreadth; and my age is nothing before thee: VERILY EVERY MAN AT HIS BEST STATE IS ALTO-GETHER VANITY." V-11b says, "Surely every man is vanity." The word "vanity" is found over 30 times in the book of Ecclesiastes and means VAIN, every time. Like LUST, every human being possesses a certain amount of VANITY, and only the Holy Spirit can control it.

181

We are told in verse 8 to remember the days of darkness, for all those who live for life under the sun only, and apart from God. Here in verse nine we are told to bear in mind, at the end of this earthly life, we must all stand before God in judgement. *Eccl. 12:14; Heb. 9:27.*

V-9.   *"Rejoice, O young man, in thy youth;"*

We are told in *Prov. 15:13* that, "A merry heart maketh a cheerful countenance: but by sorrow of-the heart the spirit is broken."

Prov. 17:22 says, "A merry heart doeth good like a medicine: but a broken spirit drieth the bones." We must realize that in our youth we are casily influenced for good or evil, and especially evil.

Young people are vulnerable to the attacks of evil spirits, and because of this we are told to "train up a child in the way he is to go, and when he is old he will not depart from it. *Prov. 22:6.*

This is the time to rejoice in serving God, while we still have our strength and energy.

We have a great example of youthful service for God in the person of Josiah in *II Chron. 34:1-7*. This youngster was made king at eight years of age, and V-3 tells us that when he had reigned 8 years that "He began to seek after the God of David his father." V-1 tells us that he reigned 31 years and.done that which was right in the sight of God.

"... and let thy heart cheer thee in the days of thy YOUTH, and walk in the ways of thine heart, and in the sight of thine eyes:"

In *I Kings 18:12b* Obadiah said to Elijah, "I thy servant fear the Lord from my youth." The word "fear" as used here means a healthy respect for God and his word.

A young person whose eyes are fixed on Jesus, will do great things for God. Jeremiah could say of the Israelites, in *Jer. 3:4b*, "My Father, thou art the guide of my youth."

I am concerned about the youth of our day, that they are in the same category as *Prov. 7:7*, which reads, "I discerned among the youths, a young man VOID of understanding." Most young people today, don't have a clue about this life or the next.

Isaiah faced this same problem in his day, for he said in *Isa. 40:30*, "Even the youths shall faint and be weary, and young men shall utterly fall." BUT V-31 says, "But they that wait upon the Lord shall renew their strength; they shall mount up with wings as eagles; they shall run, and not be weary; they shall walk and not faint."

A young person whose eyes are fixed on Christ Jesus will have no fear of the last part of this phrase.
"... but know thou, that for all these things God will bring thee into judgement."

I believe this type of Christian, who walks with the Lord, will hear the comforting words, "Well done thou good and faithful servant; thou hast been faithful over a few things, I will make thee ruler over many things: ENTER THOU INTO THE JOY OF THE LORD."

We learned from V-9 and *Ch. 12:14* that regardless of our station in life. whether saved or lost, good or bad, we must face God in judgement. We are told this in *Rom. 14:11-12*. Paul said, "For it is written, As I live, saith the Lord, every knee shall bow to me, and every tongue shall confess to God." V-12, "So then every one of us shall give account of himself to God." A sobering thought.

V-10. *"Therefore remove sorrow from thy heart, and put away evil from thy flesh:"*

It seems to me that the last part of this phrase would take care of the first part; as evil works mostly in the flesh, and that victory over the old flesh would keep a lot of sorrow out of the heart. The word of God has an awful lot to say about the flesh, for that is where the old nature, or the old man lives. There are two key words

183

here in this part of verse 10. There is sorrow and then there is flesh. Lets take a closer look at both:

1. SORROW: It has a good and a bad side to it. God told the woman in Eden in *Gen. 3:16* that he would GREATLY multiply her sorrow in childbirth, and that her husband would rule over her. FOR HER, THAT WAS THE BAD PART. The GOOD part would come when she held that infant in her arms and gazed into its eyes for the first time. Our Lord verified this in *John 16:21* when Jesus said, "A woman when she is in travail hath sorrow, because her hour is come: but as soon as she is delivered of the child, she remembereth no more the anguish, for joy that a man is born into the world." (EVEN THOUGH IN A FEW YEARS SHE WILL WANT TO PINCH HIS HEAD OFF)

    Likewise Adam would have to toil and sweat to make a living, according to *Gen. 3:17-19* but when he sat down at the table, loaded with good things to eat, the sorrow disappeared shortly. In *II Cor. 7:9-11* Paul speaks of "Godly sorrow" and "sorrow of the world." One brought salvation, the other brought death. But this should cause us to rejoice in *Rev. 21:4* which says, "And God will wipe away all tears from their eyes; and there shall be no more death, neither *sorrow*, nor crying, neither shall there be any more pain: for the former things are passed away."

2. Next lets think about the flesh for a moment:

    The word "flesh" is found hundreds of times in the Scriptures. God honored the flesh, when he made man in his image. Though he himself is Spirit, he still made man in his own image. *Gen. 1:26.* This makes man the highest order of creation. In fact the Bible speaks of "one flesh" which denotes the harmony between two people, where they become one body. Paul uses these words to show the union of Christ to his body, the church, in *Eph. 5:25,30,31.*

BUT something happened in the garden of Eden that adversely affected the flesh of all mankind. Paul explains what happened in *Rom. 5:12, 17-19; Rom. 7:5 and Rom. 8:3-8,12,13.* We can blame the flesh for every problem we have in this life.

"... for childhood and youth are vanity."

We are encouraged to take care of this body from our youth. Because of vanity and peer-pressure, we are prone to do things in the flesh that later brings sorrow and heart-ache.

After all it is a very short span from childhood to adulthood, and vanity accompanies us along the way.

Chapter 12

V-1.   *"Remember now thy Creator in the days of thy youth,"*

To remember God as Creator is to guard against the vanity of the mind. If we keep the Lord in his rightful place in our thoughts and hearts, it will protect us from over-indulgence in sinful pleasures that young people are susceptible. It is the greatest absurdity and ingratitude imaginable to give the cream and flower of life to the devil, and to leave the left-overs, the chaff, and the dregs of our life for God, who created us. Paul warns us in *II Tim. 2:22* to, "Flee youthful lusts: but follow righteousness, faith, charity, peace, with them that call on the Lord out of a pure heart." Then in *I Tim. 4:12* the Apostle said, "Let no man despise thy youth; but be thou an example of the believers, in word, in conversation, (I need an interpreter to understand what young people are talking about today) in charity, in spirit, in faith, in purity." Paul pretty well covers all bases in this verse.

"... while the evil days come not, nor the years draw nigh, when thou shalt say, I have no pleasure in them."

Lam. 3:27 tells us, "It is good for a man that he bear the yoke in his youth." *Prov. 22:6* says, "Train up a child in the way he is to go: and when he is old, he will not depart from it."

While the evil days come not means, BEFORE they come, or, be prepared for they will come. There is an old saying, "an ounce of prevention is worth a pound of cure." This is a good place to apply that saying.

It is a fact that old age brings about biological changes in the human body that affects every area of our life.

We have an illustration of this truth in *II Sam. 19:35*. A man by the name of Barzillia said to David his king, "I am this day fourscore (80) years old: and can I discern between good and evil? can thy servant taste what I eat or what I drink? (he had lost his sense of taste) can I hear any more the voice of singing men and singing women? (he had lost his sense of hearing) wherefore then should thy servant be yet a burden to my lord the king?"

There comes a time in every life, sooner in some than others, when there is no pleasure left in this life, and we are ready to depart for the next life.

The great Apostle Paul came to this time in his life, when he said to young Timothy in *II Tim. 4:6-8,* "For I am now ready to be offered, the time of my departure is at hand." *V-7,* "I have fought a good fight, (he wrung every bit of life out of his earthly journey that he possibly could) I have finished my course, (a chosen manner of conducting one self) [this word also means a point on a compass] I have kept the faith:" *V-8,* "Henceforth there is laid up for me a crown of righteousness, which the Lord, the righteous judge, shall give me at that day: and not to me only, but to all them also that love his appearing."

In verse one the preacher encourages us to seek the Lord early in life, that we might be prepared when and if dark and troublesome days come upon us.

V-2.   *"While the sun, or the light, (from the sun) or the moon, or the stars, be not darkened, nor the clouds return after the rain:"*

I disagree with those who interpret this verse as pertaining to the continued decaying of the physical human body. I believe this and following verses are typical of the calamities coming upon the earth at some future date, to vindicate God's wrath against all ungodliness. We are warned to "REMEMBER NOW THY CREATOR" that when these days come, we will be prepared to escape the judgement and wrath of a just God. There

188

are many scriptures that tell us the sun, moon, and stars will cease to function in their normal way, and will be moved out of their original orbit. *Isa. 5:30; 13:10*. In *Rev. 6:12:14* when the sixth seal is opened, there is total anarchy upon the earth.

Joel tells us in *Joel 2:10,31* and *3:15* of these calamities which take place during the "Great Tribulation" which follows the rapture of the saints. Our Lord himself said in *Matt. 24:29*, "Immediately after the tribulation of those days shall the sun be darkened, and the moon shall not give her light, and the stars shall fall from heaven, and the powers of the heavens shall be shaken."

In *Rev. 8:12* at the sounding of the fourth Trumpet, we are told, "And the fourth angel sounded, and the third part of the sun was smitten, and the third part of the moon, and the third part of the stars; so as the third part of them was darkened, and the day shone not for a third part of it, and the night likewise."

What is the significance of the phrase "nor the clouds return after the rain." We know that clouds forecast rain, which refreshes the earth. Typically speaking,-the Holy Spirit, through the grace of God refreshes the christian, and verifies that we are living under the reign of grace. But we also know that one day the influence of the Holy Spirit as we know it, will be taken from the earth, as we are told in *II Thes. 2:7*, where we read, "For the mystery of iniquity doth already work: only he who now letteth will let, until he be taken out of the way." In other words, after the reign of GRACE has ended, there will be no need of the clouds which announce the refreshing rain, which typifies the reign of grace, or, the age of grace.

When the dispensation of grace has ended, the tribulation period will follow. Then comes the kingdom age, which will be followed by the age of ages, or, the eternal age, which will never change. We will then have a new heaven and a new earth, wherein dwelleth righteousness. *II Pet. 3:13.*

If, as some commentaries suggest, that these first few verses refer to the continued decaying of the human body, how do they reconcile verses 3-7 to this concept? On the other hand, if we understand verses 1 and 2 to mean we are to remember the Creator, so that when troublous times come, we will be prepared, then it makes sense. V-9 of the previous chapter is speaking of judgement. AND we dare not forget that evil days are here now. In the tribulation period there will be great consternation over all the earth; when man will be amazed and bewildered, at the power and wrath of the Sovereign God.

V-3.   *"In the day when the keepers of the house will tremble,"*

I understand this and following verses to be a dire warning to all mankind to escape the wrath of the Almighty God, which will affect all of creation. In *Rev. 6:12-17* we find the worlds greatest prayer meeting when God's wrath is poured out on all of mankind, from kings to bondmen. Read *Rev. 14:19-20; and Rev. 16:1,18-19.*

I believe the "keepers of the house" refer to the leaders around the world, who are the "kings of the earth, and the great men, and the rich men, and the chief captains, and the mighty men" mentioned in *Rev. 6:15.* This passage speaks of a time when all men will TREMBLE with fear. *Psa. 99:1* tells us, "The Lord reigneth; let the people tremble: He sitteth between the cherubims; let the earth be moved."

In *Dan. 6:26* King Darius made a decree, that in every dominion of his kingdom, men would tremble and fear the God of Daniel.

"... and the strong men shall bow themselves,"

Because they are strong in the wrong way, as *Prov. 18:11* says, "The rich man's wealth is his strong city, and as a high wall in his own conceit." God knows how to handle this type person, for Mary told Elizabeth in *Luke 1:51-52*, "He (God) hath shewed strength with his arm; he hath scattered the proud in the imagination of their hearts." V-52, "He hath put down the mighty from their seats, and exalted them of low degree."

"*... and the grinders cease because they are few,*"

This phrase before us is the only place the word "grinders" is used, in the entire Bible. The word "grinding" is only found twice, here in V-4 and in *Matt. 24:41* (beside *Luke 17:35* which speaks of the same event as Matthew is writing about). THEREFORE, it is difficult to determine exactly what Solomon is referring to, here in V-3.

"The grinders cease because they are few," I believe refers to those who produce food staples to sustain life. We know that is what *Matt. 24:41* is talking about. It also fits here.

At the rapture many will be taken from the mills, factories, and all walks of life, therefore the production of all materials, including food products will be greatly affected.

"*... and those that look out of the windows be darkened.*"

I believe the darkness referred to here is spiritual darkness, and means that the one looking out the window is in darkness. The window itself is dark, and he is looking into the darkness outside the window. There is much said about darkness in the word of God; for instance *Isa. 5:30* predicts a day of darkness, and *Isa. 9:19* tells us, "Through the wrath of the Lord of hosts is the land darkened, and the people shall be as the fuel of the fire: no man shall spare his brother."

Speaking of darkness:

The LAND will be darkened; *Isa. 9:19.*

The EYE will be darkened; *Zech. 11:17.*

The HEART will be (or is) darkened; *Rom. 1:21.*

The UNDERSTANDING will be darkened; *Eph. 4:18.*

Lastly Paul, speaking of the days in which he lived said in *I Cor. 13:12,* "For now we see through a glass darkly."

Judgement is coming! REMEMBER THE CREATOR.

We are continuing the thought and interpretation, that the darkness in these verses mean spiritual darkness that will, one day, come upon the earth, and that Solomon is warning readers of the judgement in this last chapter.

V-4.   *"And the doors be shut in the streets,"*

I believe this has to do with fear, which will come upon the earth, and those who have trampled under foot the blood of Christ. As a matter of fact, God told Isaiah in *Isa. 63:3* that he would trample them if his fury. Then in *Exod. 15:16a* he told them, "Fear and dread would fall upon them. This fear is not to be confused with the fear of the Lord, which is the beginning of wisdom mentioned in *Psa. 111:10;* and *Prov. 9:10,* and the beginning of knowledge in *Prov. 1:7,* which means a healthy respect for the Godhead and which all christians must have. We are told in *Heb. 11:7* that Noah had this kind of respect and obedience to God. The fear that is referred to in our text, is that mentioned in *I Chron. 16:30; Psa. 96:9,* and culminating in the fear of *Rev. 21:8.*

"... when the sound of the grinding is low,"

We are told in *Jer. 25:10,* "Moreover I will take from them the voice of mirth, and the voice of gladness, the voice of the bridegroom, and the voice of the bride, the sound of the millstones, (grinding) and the light of the candle." I believe the grinding has reference to the production of food and other life-sustaining products, which will one day cease.

"... and he shall rise up at the voice of the bird,"

We have here a scene of men crouching behind locked doors, gripped with fear and trembling.

In *Isa. 13:19,21,22* we find the prophesy of the destruction of Babylon, which had become the dwelling

192

place of unclean birds and beasts. John describes this scene again in *Rev. 18:2.*

The Bible talks about clean and unclean birds, but all birds have one thing in common, they are cautious creatures, and take flight at the least provocation. God said it would be this way in *Gen. 9:2a*, "The fear of you (man) and the dread of you shall be upon every beast of the earth, and upon every fowl of the air."

We understand from these scriptures that God will use the fowls of heaven, and the beasts of earth to help carry out his vengeance on sinful man in the last days. Here in our text, he will use birds to warn man.

"... and all the daughters of music shall be brought low;"

The devil's music is doing its dirty work in the world today. However there is coming a day when his music will cease to influence and plague humanity.

We read in *Luke 23:28*, "But Jesus turning unto them said, Daughters of Jerusalem, weep not for me, but weep for yourselves, and for your children."

We have been reminded by Solomon of the fear and calamities coming upon the earth one day, and I believe, in the near future. I am convinced that verse 5 continues this line of reasoning,

V-5.   *"Also when they shall be afraid of that which is high,"*

That which is high is that which will bring the daughters of music low, for that which is high means the MOST HIGH GOD.

In its use here, the word "high" means exalted in rank or dignity, as God told Israel he would do for them if they kept his commandments. *Deut. 26:18-19.* BUT when man raises himself to this exalted state, *apart from God*, then God knows how to bring him down. *Psa. 18:2;62:9; 101:5; Prov. 21:4; Ezek. 21:25-26.*

Being afraid of that which is high is illustrated in *Isa. 6:1-5* and *Isa. 10:12,33*. When Isaiah saw the Lord high and lifted up, it changed his life completely. 37

times, from Numbers to Acts, God is referred to as "THE MOST HIGH GOD". And this is his rightful place, for in *Acts 7:48* Luke said, "Howbeit the most High dwelleth not in temples made with hands; as saith the prophet." See *Isa. 66:1* and hold that place.

"... and fears shall be in the way,"

Now look in *Isa. 66:4* where God told Isaiah, "I also will choose their delusions, (II Thess. 2:11) and will bring their fears upon them; because when I called, none did answer; when I spake, they did not hear: but they did evil before mine eyes, and chose that in which I delighted not." Now for this same reason, God will send fear and restlessness upon the earth, and when that fails to get men's attention, he will send destruction.

Paul knew what fear and trouble meant, for he said in *II Cor. 7:5*, "For when we were come to Macedonia, our flesh had to rest, but we were troubled on every side; without were fightings, within were fears."

"... and the almond tree shall flourish, and the grasshopper shall be a burden, and desire shall fail:"

At this particular time, the judgement of God is upon man, and nature is still performing as designed by the Creator. The almond tree blooms and produces almonds at God's command, not man's. This truth is beautifully illustrated in *Num. 17:1-8.*

We know from scripture that the grasshopper is an instrument of destruction, which the Lord has used many times, to bring man to his knees. When these pesky insects come through in swarms, they leave every thing in their wake barren and wasted.

We learn from *Judges 6:5* that they are associated with destruction. "And desire shall fail" means everything man tries to do will be to no avail. We read in *Psa. 10:3*, "For the wicked boasteth of his hearts desire, and blesseth the covetous, whom the Lord abhoreth." *Prov.*

194

21:25 says, "The desire of the slothful killeth him; for his hands refuse to labour."

"*... because man goeth to his long home, and the mourners go about the streets:*"

The long home refers to the grave, as Job said in *Job 17:13*, "If I wait the grave is mine house: I have made my bed in the darkness." Man's desires shall fail because death overtakes him before they are fulfilled. *Jer. 4:26-28* describes a scene of desolation at the hands of God. Yet the world of religionists thinks God never gets angry.

We have been discussing judgement upon mankind while nature continues on its intended course, but we also know that in due time, all of creation will be affected by the Divine judgement of God. In verse five the "long home" refers to the grave at death, verse six and seven continues this thought.

V-6.   "*Or ever the silver cord be loosed,*"

Remember we are discussing death and when man goes to his long home, or grave. The soul is separated from the body. I am convinced that the "silver cord" here represents the SOUL which is eternal and is separated from the body at death. This is the meaning of the loosing of the silver cord.

This is also what Paul is talking about in II Cor. 5:6-8 and I Cor. 15: *35-50*. We also know that God uses the refining process of silver as the means of purifying his people Israel. *Zech. 13:9* tells us, "And I will bring the third part (of the remnant of Israel) through the fire, and will refine them as silver is refined, and will try them as gold is tried: they shall call on my name, and I will hear them: I will say, It is my people: and they shall say, The Lord is my God."

The silver cord represents the soul bearing the body with the life thereof as *Gen. 2:7* tells us. When the silver cord is loosed, the soul goes one way and the body goes another. I see a correlation between this concept and *I Cor. 3:12-13.*

195

"... or the golden bowl be broken,"

Basically the same meaning as the loosing of the silver cord. The golden bowl represents the SPIRIT of man, which also departs the body at death. Gold is a precious metal, but so are the vessels of God which do his work. *Isa. 52:11* says, "Depart ye, depart ye, go ye out from thence, touch no unclean thing; go ye out of the midst of her; BE YE CLEAN, THAT BEAR THE VESSELS OF THE LORD."

"... or the pitchers be broken at the fountain."

The pitcher, here, is representative of the body which until death is constantly filled and emptied during our lives. BUT at death the fountain or flow of life which is in the blood, stops and the pitcher is broken off from the fountain which is God. In *Jer. 2:13* God told Jeremiah, "For my people have committed two evils; they have forsaken me the fountain of living waters, and hewed them out cisterns, broke cisterns, that can hold no water."

Zech. 13:1 tells us God is that fountain, "In that day there shall be a fountain opened to the house of David and to the inhabitants of Jerusalem for sin and for uncleanness."

"... or the wheel broken at the cistern."

A cistern is a man-made reservoir to hold water, and needs a windless or wheel with a rope running through it to draw water up out of the cistern. If the wheel is broken, then you have a problem, but I think we could safely say that all of these things, the silver cord, the golden bowl, pitcher, fountain, wheel, and cistern, represents life from God to man and back to God.

God gives life, and He can take it any time He so desires.

In verse one we are reminded to remember the Creator. To remember the Creator is to guard against the vanity of the mind, and remembering God helps to guard against the indulgence of sinful pleasures that plague young and old alike.

V-7.   *"Then shall the dust return to the earth as it was:"*

The word "dust" here is what our physical bodies are made of, and it ought to humble man when he realizes that he is made out of dirt.

Eccl. 3:20 tells us, "All go to one place, and all turn to dust again." (basically we are all dirtbags).

Gen. 2:7 tells us God formed man out of the dust of the ground, and

Gen. 3:19 tells us we will return to the dust of the ground.

Job 34:15 says, "All flesh shall perish together, and man shall turn again unto dust."

Psa. 103:29 says, "For he (God) knoweth our frame; he remembereth that we are dust." In *104:29* we read, "Thou hidest thy face, they are troubled: thou takest away their breath, they die, and return to their dust."

"... and the spirit shall return unto God who gave it."

When God breathed into Adam's nostrils the breath of life, it was a part of the Creator himself. It was His life that he gave Adam, and in so doing he brought soul and spirit together and put them in this new body that he had fashioned with his own hands, in His own image. The spirit and flesh are two separate parts of the body. Jesus warned his apostles in *Matt. 26:41* to "Watch and pray, that ye enter not into temptation: the spirit indeed is willing, but the flesh is weak."

In *Acts 7:59* it is stated,"And they stoned Stephen, calling upon God, (he was praying) and saying, Lord Jesus, receive my spirit." He knew there was about to be a separation of his spirit from his body.

According to *Eccl. 3:21*, there is the spirit of man, and the spirit of beasts, but there is a difference in the two. One goes up, the other goes down into the earth, which is the end of that animal. God does not deal with the animal spirit as he does with the human spirit. Nowhere in the Bible is there any mention of a resurrection of animal life. On the other hand, *Job 32:8* tells us, "But there is a spirit in man: and the inspiration of the ALMIGHTY giveth them understanding." It is true that animals have intelligence; some more than people, seemingly, but their spirit is not eternal.

Job 32:9 says, "Great men are not always wise: neither do the aged understand judgement." We understand that wisdom comes from God, and if man's spirit is not in harmony with God's spirit, wisdom goes begging. *Rom. 8:16*, "The Spirit itself beareth witness with our spirit, that we are the children of God." To be complete, man must have body, soul, and spirit. Each have a different function, and each have (or can have) a different place to go at death. For instance, the soul and spirit of the unsaved do not go to heaven. Paul said in *II Cor. 5:8* that for a Christian to be absent from the body, is to be present with the Lord. Where does the soul and spirit of the lost person go? The same place the rich man found himself in *Luke 16:22-23*, "The rich man also died, and was buried; and in HELL he lift up his eyes, being in torments, and seeth Abraham AFAR off, and Lazarus in his bosom."

This may be one reason for Paul's prayer for the Thessalonians in *1 Thess. 5:23*, where he prayed that their whole spirit, soul, and body be preserved blameless at the coming of the Lord.

The body, soul and spirit, each have their separate place to go at death; and we are told that they do separate.

In *Gen. 35:18* we read of Rachel's death, at the birth of Benjamin, "And it came to pass, as her soul was departing, (for she died) that she called his name Benoni, but his father called him Benjamin."

In verse seven we learned of the final destiny of this earthly body; or as Paul said in *II Cor. 5:1*, "Our earthly house of this tabernacle were dissolved." (turned back to dust) In this same verse, we have the promise that "We have a building of God

198

(after all, he built the first one. *Gen. 2:7*), an house not made with hands (anything hands build is temporary), ETERNAL IN THE HEAVENS."

V-8.   *"Vanity of vanities, saith the preacher; all is vanity."*

The book of Ecclesiastes starts with this statement in *Ch. 1:2*. The word "vanity" will be found 37 times throughout the book. This word "vanity" is a KEY word, in the study of Ecclesiastes, and represents man apart from God, or "under the sun," which is found some 29 times. I believe we can truly say that this phrase depicts man trying to find purpose and direction for his life, without God and the Son of God. The word "vanity" comes from the word VAIN, and means empty, worthless, conceited, and inflated ego. *Psa. 94:11* tells us that all mankind is affected (or infected) with this malady; and as I said back in *Ch. 1:2*, WITH SOME IT IS AN INCURABLE DISEASE.

David said in *Psa. 94:11*, "The Lord knoweth the thoughts of man, that they are vanity." You see, God has man's number!

We read in *Isa. 64:6*, "But we are all as an unclean thing, and all our righteousnesses are as filthy rags; and we all do fade as a leaf; and our iniquities, like the wind, have taken us away." The words VAIN and VANITY are found many times in the Bible, and I am sorry to say, that both are prevalent in every church across America today.

Even sadder still, is the fact that many preachers not only preach vanity, but practice it, which make their listeners vain, according to *Jer. 23:16*. Jeremiah says, "Thus saith the Lord of hosts, Hearken NOT unto the words of prophets that prophesy unto you: THEY MAKE YOU VAIN: (when they tell you how good you are, when you are living in open sin) they speak a vision of their own heart, and not out of the mouth of the Lord."

Isa. 5:20 says, "Woe unto them that call evil good, and good evil; that put darkness for light, and light for darkness; that put bitter for sweet, and sweet for bitter."

In *Matt. 15:7-9* we find Jesus rebuking the scribes and Pharisees for this very thing. He said, "Ye hypocrites, well did Esaias prophesy of you, saying, This people draweth nigh unto me with their mouth, and honoureth me with their lips: but their heart is far from me. But in VAIN do they worship me, teaching for doctrine the commandments of men." Then in *Mark 7:7* Jesus said, "Howbeit in VAIN do they worship me, teaching for doctrines the commandments of men."

It is in the vanity of his mind that man turns to idols and "diviners" for peace of mind. God's word condemns this very thing in many places. We have an example in *Zech. 10:2* which says, "For the idols have spoken vanity, and the diviners (fortune tellers) have seen a lie, and have told false dreams; *they comfort in vain*: because there was no shepherd." Paul speaks of those who had believed in vain in *I Cor. 15:2*.

So we understand from Scripture that it is possible to both believe and worship in vain, or in an empty and worthless, meaningless way.

One of the great lessons that Solomon learned, is found in V-8; that apart from God, man is altogether a vain creature. BUT in the last six verses of the book, his plea is for man to FEAR GOD AND KEEP HIS COMMANDMENTS. (V-13).

V-9.   *"And moreover, because the preacher was wise, he still taught the people knowledge;"*

Solomon is referring to himself when he says "because the preacher was wise." In the very first chapter and verse 13 he said, "I gave my heart to seek and search out by wisdom concerning all things that are done under heaven." Then in V-16 he tells us he had "gotten *more wisdom* than all that have been before me in Jerusalem: Yea my heart had great experience of wisdom and knowledge." See *I Kings 4:29 and 5:12*

200

Solomon knew from experience the whole spectrum of life; the good and bad side of it, and testifies to the fact in *Eccl. 1:17*, where he said, "And I gave my heart to know *wisdom*, and to know *madness* and *folly*: I perceived that this also is vexation of the spirit." (his spirit) Throughout this book of Ecclesiastes Solomon passes on to all who are interested, the things he has learned about life; therefore this book is the most informative book in all the Bible, about everyday life, here on earth. Like many other books in the Bible, the devil has blinded the minds of people, to keep this book hidden. It comes to close to home and heart for most people, by making them uncomfortable in their sins. See *II Cor. 4:3-4*.

"... yea, he gave good heed, and sought out, and set in order many proverbs."

Notice carefully the wording here "yea, he gave good heed." MEANING, he paid attention to learning,

Psa. 119:9 both asks and answers the question, "Wherewithal shall a young man cleanse his way? by taking heed (paying attention) thereto according to thy word."

Paul tells us in *Heb. 2:1*, "Therefore we ought to give the more *earnest heed* to the things which we have heard, lest at any time we should let them slip."

"... and sought out" meaning he searched for truth, as opposed to *Eccl. 7:29,* where we are told, that man has "sought out many inventions" to keep from serving God. Listen to *Psa. 64:6* where we read, "They (man) search out iniquities; they accomplish a diligent search: BOTH in the inward thought of every one of them, and the heart is deep."

It all started in *Gen. 3:6-7* in the eating of the forbidden fruit, and the sewing of the fig leaves, to hide their nakedness.

In *John 5:39* Jesus tells us to "search the scriptures;" and in *Acts 17:11* the Bereans " searched the scriptures daily, whether those things that Paul and Silas were teaching) were so." The result of this daily study is seen in V-12, which says "Therefore many of them believed."

I Pet.1:10 tells us the "Prophets inquired and searched diligently" the way of salvation through grace. It was a new concept to them and they wanted to know the way of it.

"... *and set in order many proverbs.*"

Proverbs are moral sayings; wise counsel, which we as christians would do well to pay attention to.

I would call the proverbs of scripture, wisdom in a nutshell. Straight to the heart of the matter.

In order to teach the people knowledge, and set in order many proverbs, Solomon sought words that the common man could understand. Paul had this same concept in mind when he said in *I Cor. 2:1*, "And I, brethren, when I came to you, came NOT with excellency of speech or of wisdom, declaring unto you the testimony of God." The man of God should not try to enhance the word of God with his own eloquence.

V-10. *"The preacher sought to find out acceptable words:"*

Solomon wanted to make sure the message would be understood by those interested enough to study them. The word of God is plain and to the point, and should be preached that way. Paul said in *I Cor. 2:4*, "And my speech and my preaching was NOT with enticing words of man's wisdom, but in demonstration of the Spirit and of power." The reason is given in *V-5*, "That your faith should not stand in the wisdom of men, but in the power of God."

In *Hab. 2:2* God told Habakkuk to, "Write the vision; and make it *plain upon tables*, that he may run that readeth it."

In *Deut. 27:8* God told Moses to tell the people of Israel to, "Write upon the stones (tables of stone) all the words of this law *very plainly.*"

In *II Cor. 3:12* Paul said, "Seeing then that we have such hope, we use great *plainness of speech*." But this word "acceptable" has another meaning, and I am sure the preacher wanted to use it in this sense also. It has the meaning of *well pleasing*, that is, well pleasing and ACCEPTABLE unto God, as Paul said in *Rom. 14:18*, "For he that in these things serveth Christ is ACCEPTABLE to God, and approved of men."

As *Eph. 5:10* says, "Proving what is acceptable unto God." So Solomon sought words that man could understand, and yet be pleasing to God.

"... *and that which was written was upright, even words of truth.*"

It sounds like the preacher found those "acceptable words" because that which was written was UPRIGHT. This word "upright" has several meanings: it not only means straight up, or vertical, or erect posture, but it also means "marked by strong moral rectitude, or principals." It means honorable, and suggests a firm holding to codes of RIGHT BEHAVIOR. I believe we could rightly say that this is what the book of Ecclesiastes is all about. It is a guide toward a high sense of honor and duty for every believer. *Prov. 10:9* says, "He that walketh UPRIGHTLY walketh surely: but he that perverteth his ways shall be known." *Prov. 28:18*, "Whoso walketh uprightly shall be saved: but he that is perverse in his ways shall fall at once." *Prov. 15:8* says, "The sacrifice of the wicked is an abomination to the Lord: but the *prayer of the upright is his delight.*"

Lets think about the last phrase of this verse, "*even words of truth.*" We are living in a day when truth is taken far to lightly. We are facing times such as Isaiah faced when he penned the words of *Isa. 59: 4,14-15*.

Psa. 51:6 tells us that God desires "truth in the inward parts."

Prov. 23:23 encourages us to "buy truth, and sell it not; also wisdom, and instruction, and understanding."

We believe every word in this book we call the Bible, is true. *John 17:17* tells us that we are sanctified through the truth of God's word. He said, "Sanctify them through thy truth: thy word is truth." May we be able to pray as David prayed in *Psa. 86:11*, "Teach me thy way, O Lord; I WILL WALK IN THY TRUTH; unite my heart to fear thy name."

The preacher sought suitable words to express his thoughts on living life here on earth, or, UNDER THE SUN. Also how to be "upright" with God and man. He has found them, as we have learned from the study of Ecclesiastes over the last 2 1/2 years. This book cannot be surpassed, for instruction, in practical living for every child of God.

V-11.   *"The words of the wise are as goads,"*\

The word "goad" means a sharp instrument, wood or metal, used to prod animals to keep them moving in the right direction, as an ox goad. This word also means to urge, or to stimulate to action. I am convinced this is Solomon's purpose in this last chapter.

In *Prov. 1:5-6* we read, "A wise man will hear, and will increase learning; and a man of understanding shall attain unto wise counsels." *V-6*, "To understand a proverb, and the interpretation; the words of the wise and their dark sayings." *Prov. 22:17*, "Bow down thine ear, and hear the words of the wise, and apply thine heart unto my knowledge." From the scriptures we learn that the goad had another use; for in *Judges 3:31*, there was a Judge by the name of Shamgar, who used a goad to kill 600 men.

I believe we find the proper rendering of the word in *Acts 2:37*, where Peter is preaching on the day of Pentecost, and it says, "Now when they heard this, they were *pricked in their hearts*, and said unto Peter and the rest of the Apostles, Men and brethren what shall we do?" Peter tells them what to do in the next verse, and in

V-41 we are told that 3,000 souls were saved. The WORD of GOD was the GOAD that moved people to action. BUT does it ever move us?

"*... and as nails fastened by the masters of assemblies, which are given from one shepherd.*"

There is an interesting passage of scripture in *Zech. 10:4*, where our Lord is called the "corner"; the "nail"; and the "battle bow." In *Isa. 22:23*, speaking of Christ, God told Isaiah, "And I will fasten him as a NAIL in a sure place; and he shall be for a glorious throne to his father's house." *V-24* says, "And they shall hang upon him all the glory of his father's house, the offspring and the issue, all vessels of small quantity, from the vessels of cups, even to all the vessels of flagons."

What we find here then, is that the "word of truth," which includes every word of SCRIPTURE. BUT, especially, the words of this book, are meant to GOAD us to active service, for our Lord; but also words that FASTEN us to Christ in that service. We are told in *Isa. 40:11* that, "He (the Lord God of V-10) shall feed his flock like a shepherd: he shall gather the lambs in his arms, and carry them in his bosom, and shall gently lead those that are with young." Then in *Isa. 44:28*, God calls Syrus his shepherd. I believe the words "masters of assemblies" refer to the under shepherd or pastor, who is following the one shepherd, who is Jesus Christ. In the beautiful 23rd Psalm, David could say, "The Lord is my shepherd."

I believe he said this with all the confidence he could muster. If the "masters of assemblies" would all follow the one true shepherd, the believers would all be securely fastened to the service of Christ, as a nail driven in a sure place, and sure manner. A nail driven into lumber must be driven all of the way, flush with the surface, and slightly below surface is even better; for that's what we call setting the nail, so that it will never work loose.

A lot of so-called Christians are never SET in Christ, therefore they work loose at the friction caused by the world. READ *Matt. 13:18-23*.

Verse twelve continues the thought of verse eleven, where Solomon said the "words of the wise are as goads." Not only to move us to action, and steer us in the right direction, but they also "admonish" the righteous. This word means to express disapproval and warning, and to indicate duties or obligations. Lets examine this next phrase with this in mind.

V-12. *"And further, by these, my son, be admonished:"*

Notice who he is addressing these words to; "my son" or as a father would warn and instruct his children. This is exactly what God's word accomplishes in us, when we receive and obey it. The person who will not be warned or admonished by the heavenly Father, through the word, has a problem.

Remember *Eccl. 4:13* tells us, "Better is a poor and a wise child than an old and foolish king, who will no more be admonished." (no fool like an old fool).

In *Rom. 15:14* we are encouraged to "admonish one another." In fact, he said, "And I myself also am persuaded of you, my brethren, that ye are full of goodness, filled with all knowledge, able also to admonish one another."

In *Rom. 15:1* Paul said, "We then that are strong ought to bear the infirmities of the weak, and not to please ourselves." To me, verse one clarifies verse fourteen. ADMONISH MEANS TO WARN, and we find Paul doing this in *Acts 27:9-10*.

In *II Thess. 3:14-15* Paul instructs the Thessalonians in the treatment of a disobedient brother in Christ. *V-15* says, "Yet count him not as an enemy, but admonish him as a brother." See *I Thess. 5:12-13*.

This admonition as a wayward christian brother, is different from the admonition of a "heretic." For in *Titus 3:10* Paul tells us plainly that "a man that is an heretic after the first and second admonition reject." This is a person who believes contrary to church doctrine, and refuses to change.

"... *of making many books there is no end;*"

There are books written on every subject known to man, and much of the writing is trash. Very few books contain words of wisdom, which admonishes and helps the reader. It is said in John 21;25, concerning Christ, that if everything he did, while on earth, was written in books, the world could not contain them. What we have in the Holy Scriptures is ALL that God wanted us to have, and they need nothing added to or taken from them. Read *Rev. 22:18-19.*

In this Divine library we call the Bible, we have all the information we need to get to heaven. When we get there, we will hear "THE REST OF THE STORY." Not only that, but we will have all eternity to absorb it all. BUT for some that will not be long enough.

"... *and much study is a weariness of the flesh.*"

From this phrase we are reminded of Paul's instruction to Timothy in *II Tim. 2:15* where he said, "Study to shew thyself approved unto God, a workman that needeth not to be ashamed, rightly dividing the word of truth." The Bible is God's gold mine of truth, but like digging for gold, it is work. Searching the Scriptures is physically tiring, exhaustive work. After all, you don't find gold and precious stones lying on top of the ground. God told Israel in *Jer. 29:13*, "And ye shall seek me and find me, when ye shall search for me with all your heart."

Jesus said in *John 5:39*, "Search the scriptures; for in them ye think ye have eternal life: and they are they which testify of me." We do not have to search for him in salvation, for he searches us out. BUT, for understanding the Bible, and for knowledge, and knowing the ways of God, we MUST search the scriptures.

In verse twelve we are given the results of hearing the "conclusion" of a subject, or matter. It will bring "weariness of the flesh" because it is tiring work. Studying the scriptures for several hours, is physically exhaustive work, but it is absolutely necessary, in order to bring a subject or doctrine to its logical conclusion.

V-13.   *"Let us therefore hear the conclusion of the whole matter:"*

Mr. Webster tells us, the word "conclusion" has several meanings, one of which is "A reasoned judgement." If I understand *Isa. 1:18* correctly this is what that scripture means. There, the invitation from God to man is, "Come now, let us reason together, saith the Lord: though your sins be as scarlet, they shall be white as snow; though they be red like crimson, they shall be as wool."

God's word is very reasonable, to the spiritually minded christian. *I Cor. 2:15.* BUT it must be rightly divided according to *II Tim. 2:15.* I believe if we rightly divide the word of God, study it until it becomes work, that God the Holy Spirit will bring us to a logical conclusion. *John 14:26 and 16:13* tell us this is the work of the Holy Spirit.

I believe another means of reaching the right conclusion of a matter, pertaining to God, is to let Scripture prove Scripture, and not try to build a doctrine on one verse from the Bible. One reason for all the confusion and ignorance in the world of christiandom today, is that preachers and teachers do not study a subject through to its reasonable and logical conclusion. It is only then that they will arrive at the truth. It is amazing to me that the Sovereign God would stop to reason with sinful man.

"Fear God, and keep his commandments:"

In *Deut. 10:12* we find God's requirements for Israel to possess the promised land. Moses said, "And now, Israel, what doth the Lord thy God require of thee, but to fear the Lord thy God, to walk in all his ways, and to love him, and to serve the Lord thy God with all thy heart, and with all thy soul." I believe this is the conclusion of the matter between God and man. God created man to serve him, that man might love him, and that he in turn would love man freely, so that man would walk in all his (God's) ways. As a matter of fact, that is what the last phrase of *V-13* tells us.

"... for this is the whole duty of man."

The word "duty" means conduct or respect due our superiors. Therefore since God created man, he is far superior to man and deserves and demands our love, respect, and service. This has been the goal of Ecclesiastes, as the Preacher has instructed man on how to find and serve God in such a manner that he would reach his greatest potential.

This is the duty of the whole human race, and we are told in *Rom. 3:19* that God is the God of the Jew and the Gentile or of all mankind. However, if a large segment of humanity will not love and worship God they must come before him in judgement, as we will learn in the closing verse of the great book.

In the beginning of this closing chapter of this great book of Ecclesiastes we are encouraged to serve God in the early days of youth, that we might escape the days of those who do not serve him. Here in the last verse of the book, we are reminded of the fact that whether we do good or evil, we must all stand before the Supreme court of Heaven.

V-14. *"For God shall bring every work into judgment,"*

This word "judgment" should be considered soberly, and with a healthy respect, by every christian, because of *II Cor. 5:9-11*. BUT the same word should strike stark raving fear into the heart of every lost person. The unsaved are amply warned throughout the Bible, as to their destination, apart from God. *Eccl. 5:7; Matt. 10:28; Rev. 20:11-15;* and *Eccl. 11:9*. The words judge, judged, and judgment are found hundreds of times in the Scriptures, and applies to every part of God's creation.

209

This is one of the absolutes of the Bible, that nothing or no one is exempt from judgment. God's only begotten Son, himself, was judged by the world, on the cross.

"... *with every secret thing,*"

John 7:4a says, "For there is no man that doeth anything in secret, and he himself seeketh to be known openly." We are told in *Eph. 5:11-13*, "And have no fellowship with the unfruitful works of darkness, but rather reprove them." *V-12*, "For it is a shame even to speak of those things which are done of them in secret." *V-13*, "But all things that are reproved are made manifest by the light."

Many so-called christians are so foolish as to think they are hiding their sins from God. Even David might have thought this at some point in his life, but later learned better, for he said in *Psa. 19:12*, "Who can understand his errors? Cleanse thou me from secret faults."

Psa. 90:8 is a warning even though it is a prayer of Moses, he said, "Thou hast set our iniquities before thee, our secret sins in the light of thy countenance."

Jer. 23:24 poses an interesting question from God, "Can any hide himself in secret places that I shall not see him? saith the Lord. Do not I fill heaven and earth? saith the Lord."

Jer. 23:25 says, "I have heard what the prophets said, that prophesy LIES in my name, saying I have dreamed, I have dreamed."

Our Lord gives his feelings about this same crowd in *Matt. 7:21-23*, where he said, "Not every one that saith unto me, Lord, Lord, shall enter into the kingdom of heaven; but he that doeth the will of my Father which is in heaven." *V-22*, "Many will say to me in that day, Lord, Lord, have we not prophesied in thy name? and in thy name cast out devils? and in thy name done many wonderful works?" *V-23*, "And will I profess unto them, I never knew you: depart from me, ye that work iniquity."

"*... whether it be good, or whether it be evil.*"

This is true for saved and lost. *II Cor. 5:10* tells us the saved will suffer LOSS, but will be saved so as by fire. *I Cor. 3:15.*

For the lost, all of their good works will not keep them out of the fire, according to *Rev. 20:12-15*; even though there may be degrees in punishment. See *Jer. 21:14 and Matt. 23:14.*

In *Matt. 12:36-37* we are told that we must give an account of every idle word, and that we are justified or condemned by our words. *V-34* tells us it is "Out of the abundance of the heart that the mouth speaketh." If its not in the heart the mouth can't say it.

I believe that Solomon has taught us that in order to get the most out of life under the *S U N* we must have the life that is above the sun, which is the life of the *S O N*. May God help us to obtain it.